Career-Defining Crises
in Mission

NAVIGATING THE MAJOR DECISIONS
OF CROSS-CULTURAL SERVICE

"This book comes to our missions for just such a time as this. Today's missionaries are faced with a veritable avalanche of information, proposals, and programs that cry out for their attention. Before they become cyber-spaced out, they and their leaders should make sure that they read this book!"

Dr. David Hesselgrave
Missiologist, author, consultant
Trinity International University

"Paul Keidel's insights have been tested in the crucible of more than two decades of cross-cultural ministry. He challenges us to be wise and discerning when it comes to importing methods and money from our sending country. More important are authentic relationships opening the door for the hard work of developing healthy, reproducing followers of Jesus. This is a must-read for every cross-cultural worker."

Dr. Robert L. Fetherlin
Vice President, International Ministries
Christian and Missionary Alliance

"Veteran missionary, Paul Keidel, has zeroed in on two seemingly contradictory but perennial problems in mission praxis: (1) the cult of 'new and improved methods' that often lead missionaries away from the essential and biblical task of building relationships with people, and (2), what I would call the 'manyana syndrome' of putting off the creative engagement of one's mind with new ideas. Missionaries are notorious for falling for both, and many will find real and substantial benefit from the thoughtful antidotes that Keidel offers up."

Dr. Gary Corwin
Associate editor, *Evangelical Missions Quarterly*
Special representative, SIM International

"This book will be an asset in helping missionaries truly shift into a third gear of effectiveness in cross-cultural witness and ministry, behind impersonal methodology and strategy. It is helpful to be reminded that God calls us to relationships, and that an incarnational witness is essential in bridging the gap between cultures and making the gospel relevant and appealing. Career-Defining Crises in Mission *is a valuable resource for those responding to God's call to missionary service in understanding how to channel their passion through sensitive and practical identification with the people of the host culture."*

Dr. Jerry Rankin
President, International Mission Board
Southern Baptist Convention

Career-Defining Crises
in Mission
NAVIGATING THE MAJOR DECISIONS
OF CROSS-CULTURAL SERVICE

Paul Keidel

William Carey Library
Pasadena, California
www.WCLBooks.com

Cover design: Chris Kim
Editing: Sharon Edwards
Typesetting: Galen Currah

Published by William Carey Library
1605 E. Elizabeth Street, Pasadena, California 91104
www.WCLBooks.com

Printed in the United States of America

Library of Congress Cataloging-in-Publication Data

Keidel, Paul.
  Career-defining crises in mission : navigating the major decisions of cross-cultural service / Paul Keidel.
    p. cm.
  ISBN 0-87808-345-6 (alk. paper)
  1. Missions--Theory. 2. Christianity and culture. 3. Intercultural communication--Religious aspects--Christianity. I. Title.

  BV2063.K45 2005
  266--dc22

                              2005025823

Dedicated to the thousands of Sent-Ones

who sacrificed their lives in the 20th century

so that His Story could be told.

Contents

Figures   viii

Preface   ix

Introduction   1

Chapter

  1. The Crisis of Going Native   9

  2. The Crisis of Language   21

  3. The Crisis of the Social Gospel   35

  4. The Crisis of Telling the Story   51

  5. The Crisis of Deciding for Christ   63

  6. The Crisis of an Indigenous Church   79

  7. The Crisis of Worship and Witness   95

  8. The Crisis of Leadership   107

  9. The Crisis of Relationships with the Church   123

 10. The Crisis of Mission Transition   137

 11. The Crisis of Money and Mission   147

 12. The Crisis of Being vs. Doing   163

Appendix

  A. Check Your Fluency Progress   175

  B. Evaluating a Church's Maturity   183

Additional Reading   193

Notes   203

About the Author   211

Figures

Figure 1. Skeleton-Scaffold   131

Figure 2. Fusion-Dichotomy   131

Preface

MISSIONARIES TODAY FACE a constant barrage of new ideas and methods to help them deal with their cross-cultural decisions. They are challenged to at least be contemporary in their approach to the host cultures. Some new recruits arrive in their adopted country full of ideas, but not understanding how to choose from them. Ultimately, some fall prey to their home cultural presupposition assuring them that they have all the right methods, when they don't need a method. *Evangelical Missions Quarterly* quotes a former Yugoslavian youth pastor as saying that American missionaries, in particular, "are more or less goal oriented rather than people oriented" (October 2002:485).

Career-Defining Crises in Mission is written for the missionary in ministry. It aims to help him or her evaluate ministry approaches that bring one to relationships rather than methods. Each chapter, beginning with enculturation and continuing through descriptions of a Christ-centered assembly, leads them through Bible study, true mission stories, illustrations, and practical suggestions that will help them make decisions that lead them to interact with people before choosing methods of mission.

Career-Defining Crises in Mission brings twelve key cross-cultural problems to the reader's attention. Chapters 1 and 2 begin with the challenges of one's first cross-cultural encounter, guiding the reader through the problems faced in language learning and cultural adaptation. He is given suggestions on keeping a balance in his choices, without compromising the Message. The next chapter provides questions and analysis to guide in the use of social projects that meet the local felt need in way that enhances the Message, and avoids tying people to foreign money. Chapters 4 and 5 set forth principles for choosing effective ways of sharing the Message so that people are brought together to a decision. Chapters 6–8 reveal presuppositions and attitudes that enable the Church to be a Christ-centered movement. A refreshing definition for the indigenous church is proposed, which includes a useful tool that local church leaders can use with believers. Chapter 9 encourages the reader to step out of his present situation and evaluate the relationship that has developed with the emerging church. He will read about steps to take that will develop stronger cooperation with the church, and their faithfulness to the call to be the Church. Chapter 10 gives suggestions for transition from the established group to a new people group, and the next chapter discusses the sticky problem of money in missions, proposing guidelines for financial relationships that can help reduce the causes of money-related tension. Chapter 12 concludes with the words of Jesus to the missionary who feels obsessed with success and activity, rather than knowing Christ better.

Career-Defining Crises in Mission is written for the sent-one who is already in ministry. It takes well-known missiological principles and explains them in a missionary friendly style. Rather than focusing on heavy theory, this book helps the already busy foreign worker to revisit key cross-cultural problems, emphasizing relevant theory and its application to each situation. This book will challenge some long revered missionary values, while providing helpful suggestions.

A missionary colleague, after critiquing this manuscript, remarked, "I have to rethink some things!"

Paul R. Keidel

Introduction

What should change in your "doing mission"?

PETER HAD SWORN HE would be true to Jesus even to death, and he had already whacked off someone's ear to prove it. But when an observant servant girl recognized him as a follower of Jesus, Peter's resolve melted. Within a short span, he denied knowing Jesus three times. Then the Lord looked straight at Peter, who remembered his impetuous oath and "went out and wept bitterly" (Luke 22:60–62).

Peter failed to keep his promise and let down his best friend.

Jesus' words haunted him, and His look pierced Peter's soul.

This was a crisis of definition—what I call a career-defining crisis. It was a moment of time when Peter was forced by a crisis to see his inner self in the light of his relationship with Christ. Jesus later showed full acceptance and confidence in Peter. But Jesus' words of affirmation made more sense because Peter had first passed through the personal career-defining crisis.

Every missionary or "sent-one" has career-defining moments. His or her personal response or reaction to such events often determines the way he or she will cope with future crises. That is why it is career-defining. Let us begin by looking at the big picture of the twelve critical and defining experiences that you will likely face as a sent-one.

Into Africa

My parents sailed from New York City to Africa in the winter of 1951. Once in the Belgian Congo, they traveled by steam locomotive to the capital city of Leopoldville (now Kinshasa), and then made their way into the bush. I began my life in a grass-roofed hut. We bathed in a washtub on a hard dirt floor; a kerosene lamp showed us the way at night. Culture shock was the first crisis to define my parents' lifestyle.

My parents and their colleagues planted churches among the head hunting Bashilele people group, and learning the Bashilele language was the second crisis they faced. The Bashilele were a primitive people who, at that time, wore no more than a loincloth. Even women wore only a small cloth at the waist. Their ways were deeply rooted in witchcraft, and understanding their primitive world-view was another crisis that defined the career of the sent-ones.

The missionary team was faced with intense struggles as they sought the best way to bring Christ to this people. The Bashilele, who did not have adequate words in their language to express love, slowly discovered the Truth about God's love and chose to follow Christ. They also knew little about personal hygiene. They ate with unclean hands or drank impure water and said that evil spirits (not germs) brought disease. The courageous mission team faced the crisis of choosing the best way to demonstrate God's care for the people's well being. The Bashilele believed in the spoken word, not the written word, a crisis that defined the way the team introduced the Living Word to them. And when people began to believe the Truth of Christ, the mission team walked with believers through the maturing stages of church development, always seeking to lead them to Christ-like behavior so that the church would be the Church among the Bashilele, and not a transplant from the North America. The political turmoil in the 1990s forced the foreign missionaries to leave Congo. The heart-wrenching crisis of transition was severe as these faithful servants left their life behind. This was yet another career-defining crisis.

The twentieth century brought phenomenal changes that chal-lenged the missionary methods of our predecessors. New inventions made life easier. Jetliners replaced the long journeys by steamship. The helicopter drop-off replaced the arduous jungle trek. Electronic mail through satellite connections upstaged the telegraph. Video projections rendered preaching skills obsolete. Medical antibiotics transformed an infected limb doomed for amputation into a healthy body part. A letter could be typed without effort on a computer keyboard. Solar powered lights outshone kerosene lamps. In the midst of technical advancement, cross-cultural workers observed the birth of several mission methods, but none of the advances changed the basic struggles of "doing mission."

My wife and I went to Zaire in 1979. We lived in a remote forest region, and although our standard of living was better than that of my parents, the crises that defined our ministry were the same. We also faced culture shock, and we also had to deal with learning a strange language, and new communication styles. We had to work harmoniously with team members, both foreign and African. The way we reacted to these differences defined the direction of our ministry.

As a missionary sent-one, you face the same personal tensions in the twenty-first century. The manner in which you respond to each crisis will directly affect your success in reaching people with the Message[1] of Jesus. How will you respond? Will you withdraw in fear, or will you face each new challenge with the courage of the Holy Spirit?

As you look ahead to the new century, it is time to evaluate your ministry assumptions. You may think that your method of mission causes the tension. Think again! Do you really need a new method to communicate the Message? Or is the problem deeper? Are you asking the wrong questions when you face the stress of cross-cultural ministry?

This discussion about doing mission in difficult places came alive one time when I was visiting colleagues in a remote African town. These servants of God were frustrated because they felt that they were doing much and gaining little. In desperation, one of them said, "I feel like we are reinventing the wheel!" He may have been right. If they were trying innovations that others have employed successfully but which are now without success, perhaps they were limiting themselves. Perhaps the real crisis was that they were making incorrect choices about how to do ministry.

Many crises in cross-cultural ministry will tempt you to choose another course of action. What are the convictions that drive those choices? How do you choose what is best? This book will help you evaluate the most important choices of cross-cultural ministry.

Starting Point

Before launching into this evaluation of mission approaches, we must agree on our common starting place. Agreeing about two convictions will enable us to confront the challenges that face us.

First, we experience a powerful Message

The biblical record provides a clear explanation of God's Message. It describes how God intended for humankind to have a life of intimacy with Him, a desire that was ruined by sin. But God, being rich in love, provided a solution to the problem, giving His Son to restore the broken relationship. The Bible tells this Story, which promises to transform those who accept it.[2]

Because [God] himself gives all men life and breath and everything else, from one man he made every nation of men, that they should inhabit the whole earth; and he determined the times set for them and the exact places where they should live. God did this so that men would seek him and perhaps reach out for him and find him, though he is not far from each one of us (Acts 17:26–27). But we all, like sheep, have gone astray; each of us has turned to his own way (Is. 53:6–7). All of us have become like one who is unclean, and all our righteous acts are like filthy rages ... (Is. 64:6). The Lord is not slow in keeping his promise, as some understand slowness. He is patient with you, not wanting anyone to perish, but everyone to come to repentance (2 Pet. 3:9). You see, at just the right time, when we were still powerless, Christ died for the ungodly ... But God demonstrates his own love for us in this: while we were still sinners, Christ died for us (Rom. 5:6–8). For God so loved the world that he gave his one and only Son, that whoever believes in him shall not perish but have eternal life. For God did not send his Son into the world to condemn the world, but to save the world through him (John 3:16–17). In love he predestined us to be adopted as his sons through Jesus Christ ... in him we have redemption through his blood ... to bring all things in heaven and on earth together under one head, even Christ (Eph. 1:5, 7, 9, 10).

The Message is clear: we are sinners and separated from God, but because God is love, we now have hope that Christ will redeem us from our inherited and self-inflicted evil.

Second, this Message demands personal action

The hope of this Message is so powerful that it transforms our lives. Knowing this, Jesus gave His disciples a parting word of advice—His action mandate—and Pentecost would provide the spiritual motivation that would propel the disciples to tell the Story. The words of Christ's commission served as an affirmation of what was already happening in the hearts of His followers. It gave them an extra push.

> [Jesus] said to them, "Go into all the world and preach the good news to all creation. Whoever believes and is baptized will be saved ..." (Mark 16:15). He told them, "This is what is written: The Christ will suffer and rise from the dead on the third day, and repentance and forgiveness of sins will be preached in his name to all nations, beginning in Jerusalem. You are witnesses of these things. I am going to send you what my Father has promised ..." (Luke 24:45–49). But you will receive power when the Holy Spirit comes on you; and you will be my witnesses in Jerusalem, and in all Judea and Samaria, and to the ends of the earth" (Acts 1:8). Then Jesus came to them and said, "All authority in heaven and on earth has been given to me. Therefore [in going][3] make disciples of all nations, baptizing them in the name of the Father and of the Son and of the Holy Spirit, and teaching them to obey everything I have commanded you. And surely I will be with you always, to the very end of the age" (Matt. 28:18–20).

Jesus is the focus of our Message. Because we believe Him, we will tell others our story, and this will lead them to believe in Him and receive forgiveness for their sins. If they do not believe in Jesus, their sins remain against them and they are "judged already," because they have not "believed in the name of the only begotten Son of God" (John 3:18). If a message does not come from a heart committed to Jesus as the Son of God, that story may not be the Message from the Father. As John states in his first letter, "what we have seen and heard we proclaim...." (1 John 1:3).

Jesus sends you to tell the Story. When you fulfill this command, people will find forgiveness for their sins and their lives will be transformed. Over the centuries, followers of Christ have used a myriad of styles to tell His Story, but variety of methods did not change the core Message. When you are sent, it is equally important that you declare the Message without altering the meaning of the Story. Sometimes people are so enthusiastic about telling others about the hope that is within, that they forget that the manner used to tell the gospel may obscure the Truth. My desire is that this book will lead you to a careful self-examination of the ways in which you are doing mission and help you sharpen the image of Christ that you are presenting to those who don't know Him.

Your Crisis

You know the Message. It has not changed.

You obeyed Jesus' order and have gone to tell His Story. That, too, has not changed.

So what has changed?

The world is changing rapidly. As you transition into this new century, you will face the challenge of correctly choosing each step of your cross-cultural pilgrimage. When you face the crisis of cultural adaptation or learning a new language, you must learn to behave and speak in a manner that clearly proclaims the Message. When you gather people around the Christ of the Message and build them into a Christ-focused church, you must lead them to treasure the Message that still transforms hearts. When your newly planted church sends out workers of its own and you must transition to other areas of ministry, you will again face career-defining choices that will keep the Message of Christ true to its Founder.

My goal in the following chapters is to guide your thoughts to the best choices for each crisis. In doing so, I will present the values expressed by one of the greatest missionaries ever to go with the Message. The Apostle Paul put it this way:

> For the word of the cross is to them that perish foolishness; but unto us who are saved it is the power of God.... And my speech and my preaching were not in persuasive words of wisdom, but in demonstration of the Spirit and of power: that your faith

should not stand in the wisdom of men, but in the power of God" (1 Cor. 1:18; 2:1–5).

If you grasp this principle before you go, you will succeed in the host culture.

Chapter 1

The Crisis of Going Native

How deeply do you adapt to your new culture?

APPEARANCE TELLS A STORY. When you enter a new culture, do you have to change what you are as a person in order for your Message to be more attractive to the hearer? Cultural adaptation is one of the first monumental crises that you must conquer. When you leave your homeland, you are intellectually aware of new cultural adjustments, but you will probably not be emotionally ready for the effect this will have on yourself, your marriage, and your relationships. The reactions to new culture are varied. While some choose to live like the locals, others want to retreat into a fantasyland. You might well be thrown into depression because you feel trapped in this strange, perhaps horrible, new world.

Culture adjustment is a fact of cross-cultural life. You will face it because you are different! The purpose of this chapter is to help you analyze the biblical basis for "going native." My goal is to help you make decisions that enhance your ability to cope as a foreigner with your hosts. As you understand and apply these ideas, the crisis of being different from your neighbors will become more manageable.

Mary Slessor, a Sent-One Who Went Native

The English missionary, Mary Slessor (1848-1915), lived in Duke Town in the Calabar region of Nigeria, where living in the missionary community was very stressful. A cup of tea was tempting at three in the afternoon, but Mary wanted to be where the people were. After her first home assignment, she moved further inland to Old Town where she found freedom to live her way. She dressed in a simple cotton dress instead of the smothering Victorian gown, and she usually walked barefoot. She lived in a hut and ate local food.

Her accommodation was as unkempt as the native dwellings, with a collection of roaches and mice. Mary Slessor faced continuous problems with malaria and skin ailments. She spent very little of her allowance, sending most of it back to England to help her family. In spite of her spartan and less-than-sanitary lifestyle, Slessor outlived many of her contemporaries.[1]

Identifying with the people in this manner opened many doors of ministry for Mary Slessor. She operated schools during the week and carried out itinerant evangelism on weekends. Incensed by the local custom of killing newborn twins, she began to rescue these children and care for them. She also helped their mothers overcome the fear associated with keeping children whom society had rejected.

During her third term, Slessor went further up country into the Okoyong region, where male missionaries had previously been attacked. She was convinced that, as a single lady, the Okoyong people would not be threatened by her presence. Her instinct proved to be correct. She continued her ministry of rescuing twins and led an extensive evangelistic ministry, using locally trained Christian teams. As Mary continued to serve in areas where foreign men could not or would not go, she became a highly respected arbitrator in interpersonal conflicts. The British government appointed her vice-consul, and she was locally called the "White Queen."

Despite criticism from her colleagues, Mary lived as one with her people. She allowed God to use her talents and gifts to meet a spiritual need. Although her ministry did not generate any great people movement, her attitude of service impacted many lives in the Okoyong region. One African historian attests that Slessor became internationally famous, an eccentric figure who embodied in her own life the "preferential option for the poor."[2]

Biblical Models of Adaptation

The subject of "incarnational ministry" or "going native" is a controversial issue in mission circles. The disparity of wealth between the industrial world and many developing nations has increased the heat in this debate. Various passages of Scripture have been cited to support both sides of the argument, but with little actual impact on the way people do mission. A certain tension concerning the lifestyle of a non-native in a foreign culture will always exist.

Ultimately, resolution of the tension needs to be a personal decision based on personal conviction. Two passages can clarify the attitude of a Christian on this subject—Philippians 2:1–12 and 1 Corinthians 9, from which we derive two important principles.

First, empty the "I" in your soul (Phil. 2:1-12)

Paul wrote to the believers at Philippi to encourage them to work together as a body of believers and to exhort them to be like Christ in interpersonal relationships. This passage begins with "therefore," thus connecting the thoughts to the previous context, where Paul had spoken of the conflicts that the Philippians were facing. He now draws their attention to Christ, asking them to have the same mind, the same love, a united spirit, and one purpose. This is a call to unity. He further reminds them that their self-interests are not to motivate their actions. Rather, they should "have the same attitude which was also in Christ Jesus who ... emptied himself, taking on the form of a servant ..." (vv. 5–7).

This passage is often used to demonstrate that the missionary must be like Jesus, who left the glory of God to become one of us (John 1:1–4). Jesus divested Himself of the form and the visible glory of God, with all its attendant benefits, in order to become a servant to human beings. With that picture in mind, we are told that we must divest ourselves of our home culture in order to become totally integrated into a new one. We are told that we will more effectively reach the host culture when we fully go native in our lifestyle, like Jesus did. Keep in mind that Jesus had little need for cultural adaptation in order to serve His people. He was born to Jewish parents, lived with His siblings in a Jewish home, and rubbed shoulders with Jewish neighbors. At the start of His ministry, Jesus first went to the lost sheep of Israel, to His own people.

The lesson that Paul is teaching is not about cross-cultural ministry per se. Rather, it is an exhortation to demonstrate the attitude of Christ in every relationship, be it within our own culture or a different one. When all believers, whether or not they are sent-ones, emulate the attitude of Jesus, they will be in harmony with one another and with God, resulting in a more effective witness to a watching world. This is a call to the right attitude in ministry, one of total submission to the will of God, which enables us to set aside all personal interests—the "I" that often seems so important. When "I" receives its proper place, we are freed to identify with others and work better with them.

Second, seek to "win some" (1 Cor. 9)

Paul was severely criticized by the Judaizers and some converts at Corinth, who said that his method of ministry was compromising what they considered to be a Scriptural ethic. Depending on the critic, Paul was either giving up too many Jewish traditions to reach the Gentiles, or he was not doing enough. In this passage, Paul addressed three issues: his personal rights (vv.1–18), his service to all men (vv. 19–23), and his self-discipline (vv. 24–27).

The discussion centered on his behavior in the various cultural settings. The apostle repeated his primary objective as doing all "for the sake of the gospel" (v. 23). Declaring the Message was the bottom line that he would not step across. Paul was willing to forgo any personal qualm or cultural trait so that he might "save some" (v. 22). Although he would not compromise Scriptural truth or its moral code (v. 21) he had set aside personal desire and disciplined himself in every way lest, after having preached to others, he might be disqualified (v. 27). As a result of this conviction, Paul endured many kinds of hardship. For example, he laid aside the right to be married (v. 5). He considered his rights to be privileges that could or should be laid aside in order to become a partaker of God's Truth (v. 23). Ultimately, Paul's goal was not to win "all" but to win "some." He pursued a realistic expectation.

You will not win the whole nation. You may not even see a people group come to Christ. But as you live in the host culture in a Christ-like way, you will see people won to Christ.

Develop Your Convictions

As a worker in the twenty-first century, you should give special attention to your convictions regarding other cultures. If you can understand what you believe about the host culture, your reaction will not be one of shock. There are four basic principles from these texts to guide you as you face this cultural tension.

1. Proclamation takes priority

Six times in 1 Corinthians 9 Paul stated what he did in order to insure the declaration of the gospel. He was under compulsion to preach the message (v. 6). He preached without being paid, not caring as long as he could preach (v. 18). He made himself as a slave or free man, under the Law or without the Law, weak or strong, just so he might tell the Story of Christ (vv. 19–23). Paul disciplined his body so that he would not be disqualified from the prize reserved for those who have run faithfully (vv. 24–27).

Whatever happens, you are sent in order to make the truth of the gospel known. Therefore, you must be prepared to make whatever cultural adjustments are necessary to effectively proclaim the Message.

2. Material remuneration is a privilege, not a right

There is a vast difference between a privilege and a right. The person who claims to have rights views his service as basically contractual in nature. Thus, he expects remuneration. A privilege, on the other hand, is a special favor that is given on the basis of mercy and grace rather than on a bilateral contract. Paul stated in 1 Corinthians 9:3–6 that he had the right to eat, to drink, and to take along a believing wife. However, he did not insist upon these rights, if having them would hinder him from fulfilling Christ's mandate. To drive this point home, Paul gave three illustrations about the right to receive a salary (v. 7). A soldier was paid a wage to go into battle, a farmer ate the fruit of his harvest, and a shepherd, who was often a slave, received his rations. These examples were given to show that the workers received a reward for their labor, but Paul did not insist on the same right because he served under a *spiritual* principle, which focused on the proclamation of the gospel (vv. 11–12).

See your calling as a privilege. You cannot demand a salary from your supporters for you serve a higher Master, who has promised to care for you (Matt. 28:20; Luke 10:6–9; Phil. 4:13, 19). Hudson Taylor and other missionaries of the China Inland Mission modeled this attitude. Each missionary depended totally on the heavenly Father, not asking for financial help from any person. Although this method might not always be practiced today, when you are sent, serve Christ with this attitude. It will free you from the bondage of worry.

A related issue is the impact of lifestyle on the Message. In developing countries, this will either help or hinder the gospel presentation. Workers sent from the wealthy middle class of North America, Europe, and Asia are finding their perception of basic living needs increasing by leaps and bounds. There was a time when the sent-one left home with one or two trunks containing all that was needed to begin a new life. Some even packed their supplies in a casket-size crate, knowing that they would succumb to some local disease. On the contrary, it is common for a present-day worker to rent a large truck to move household goods to the next assignment. Sometimes each subsequent move requires a bigger truck! I have heard of families returning for a new ministry assignment needing six weeks to set up house, because they had brought back a seven-meter container full of possessions. Some foreign workers will not move into their house because the water heater doesn't work, and some workers hire guards to protect their homes against local bandits. They worry about leaving the place unattended in the evenings when going out to ministry opportunities, lest someone breaks in. Jonathan Bonk warns against this subtle change.

> Each succeeding generation of Western missionaries is culturally conditioned to redefine personal material "needs" according to a continually escalating standard that most of the world's population can only regard as wildly inflated ...[3]

Lifestyle concerns become the priority. The Apostle Paul's recommendation, however, is that your lifestyle is a negotiable item. You cannot count your material things as essential to the work. You should be willing to leave many things behind. Remember that wealth and possessions can negatively affect how both the ministry and the Message are perceived.

3. Do not jealously cling to a home cultural identity

This is the attitude of Jesus that Paul demonstrated—he did not insist on keeping what he possessed from birth because he did not want anything to hinder the declaration of the Story. As he reminded the Corinthian believers, he adapted himself to each culture (1 Cor. 9:17–19).

As a sent-one, hold your upbringing lightly, and let it not be something that you cling to. Understand that your cultural background frames your worldview. As a result, the decisions you make, the values you cherish, and the rights and wrongs you hold dear will reflect this background. Recognize that it is as difficult for you to relinquish your cultural traits as it is for your hosts to leave hold of theirs.

On the other hand, some missionaries are so self-conscious about their foreignness in their host culture that they try to shed all apparent home cultural accouterments. They dress like the hosts and talk like them, even using local slang without knowing its connotation! They live in the same kind of houses, and eat the same food, sometimes ignoring commonsensical cleanliness habits. They fail to realize, however, that the people they want to minister to may be so puzzled by this attempt to go native that the gospel itself becomes strange.

Your attitude toward cultural differences will also affect your choice of methods for sharing the Story. For example, if you are from a "can do" culture where no mountain is too large for the correct strategy to remove, you might plan evangelism in the same way, believing that planting churches is not difficult so long as the right methods are applied. You may find yourself seeking varieties of methods that win people to Christ in the same way that teenagers adopt a new hairstyle. In the final analysis, your evangelism process may appear to the hearer as a foreign or industrialized way of doing things.

The Apostle Paul's attitude is your model. Be willing to lay aside those cultural values and identities that hinder the hearing of the Message. Do not wear your citizenship like a flashy necktie, even if others do. You are a foreigner in this land, just as Abraham was a sojourner (Heb. 11:9). Shed any foreignness that you can divest and maintain your integrity. Accept your differentness, but accept the right points of difference so that "some might be won to Jesus."

4. Master personal desires so you can reach the ultimate goal

Paul's attitude on ministry is summarized in 1 Corinthians 9:24–27. He viewed life as a contest in which the participants were running to win. They pursued the goal of winning acclaim that was only momentary—a wreath that withered—but as an apostle, Paul aimed for an eternal prize, a heavenly laurel that was far more valuable than any earthly crown. So he beat his own body into submission, for "everyone who competes exercises self-control in all things" (v. 25). Paul put himself under the discipline needed so that after having preached to others, he might not himself be disqualified from receiving the prize (v. 27).

You are in a spiritual contest. The nature of that competition suddenly focuses when you land in the host country. As you learn about the people's worldview and ways, you will realize how quickly you make cultural mistakes, thereby becoming a hindrance to the gospel. So discipline yourself. Adapt habits of relationship and behavior that will help you to be appreciated, and avoid habits that are insulting. Learn the language so as to express yourself in as local a fashion as possible. Develop friendships that will open doors for the Message. Live in a house that meets local expectation without distancing yourself from others. Refrain from bragging about the power, wealth, and development successes of your homeland. Avoid adding material things and customs that confirm the people's expectation that being Christian is synonymous to being wealthy. Use methods that clearly communicate the gospel in a culturally acceptable fashion without placing accent on the technique, power, personality, intellect, or wealth of the messenger. Be willing to laugh at your mistakes, and maintain a forgiving attitude towards the mistakes of others. In short, live like one who is submitted to a higher and divine plan, yet with the humility of a servant.

Prepare for Culture Shock

Attitude matters! Knowing the reasons for your convictions about lifestyle will help you to cope with cross-cultural stresses. This foundation will give you a reference point as you inevitably travel the four levels of cultural adjustment. The length of time you spend on any of these four levels depends on your attitude, your flexibility, and the emotional strength you have to manage the ambiguity of new events.

1. You live in a honeymoon bubble—almost

Upon arrival, the unusual cultural differences charm you. People eat with sticks, and their food tastes exciting. Women dress in such colorful attire; the shops are full of exotic items. Living here is like being a tourist all the time. It is fun! Unfortunately, the novelty of such discoveries often creates the illusion that adapting to a new culture will be relatively easy.

It is at this point that the experienced missionary can help by introducing you to local customs, greetings, and gestures, as well as to the social or community leaders. He can help you acquire everyday living habits that will enable you to succeed in the next stage. But watch out! The honeymoon does not last very long.

2. You will crash—a crisis pops the bubble

Once the mice eat the chocolate chip cookies, or the email to your friends back home doesn't go through, or the local vendors rip you off, the newness evaporates. The honeymoon is over and tourism is as extinct as the flying dinosaur. You crash into the second stage of crisis and feel very foreign—you know you are an outsider here, *and so do they*!

Disillusionment takes over. Depression haunts your doorstep.

You cannot believe that people can tolerate living like this!

You battle with depression and regret having left a successful ministry back home.

You are angry that the mission board abandoned you.

This is a time of confusion. Frequently, psychosomatic illnesses surface—stomach disorders, persistent colds, flu, skin ailments, and unusual allergies.

Experienced colleagues can help by listening, caring, and encouraging. They should draw your attention to the progress that you are making in learning the language. They can remind you of the spiritual values that brought you here, and point to future ministry opportunities that will open as a result of cultural adaptation. All in all, as the newcomer, you need to know that others who preceded you have traveled this road too. As human beings, they were also shocked by the change.

The duration of this stage depends on your willingness to discipline yourself and be flexible with personal values. Your motivation to get on with life and ministry also determines how long it will take you to adapt.

3. You accept the differences

As you understand and accept the differences, you begin to see a ray of hope in the darkness. Progress in the new language reminds you that you will make it. As friendships with the locals begin to develop, you realize that there really is something worthy to do here. At this stage, the inconveniences of life are accepted with a degree of humor and tolerance. You begin to find a place in ministry and local people begin responding. Life begins to flow.

Experienced missionaries can help by affirming your progress and contribution. They will encourage your positive attitude, which moves you to the last stage.

4. You find your place—enculturation begins

Finally, you begin finding your position in the local ministry puzzle. You can get around on your own, without the constant aid of the experienced colleague. Your children play happily with the neighbors' kids and can probably speak the local language better than you! Life seems normal at last.

The experienced missionary should refrain from giving advice, except when asked. This final stage should be permanent. It is at this point that you will settle into the lifestyle patterned after your convictions.

Conclusion: Be Genuinely *You*

To what degree should you go all native, rejecting your birth culture and identity? To truly go native and do it well, you must deny yourself all of the home culture and its amenities. This means that you will never return to your homeland, not even in a medical emergency. You will live in the same kind of house as the locals. You will submit your children to the same educational advantages or disadvantages as other children in the local schools. You will eat the same food, sleep on the same kinds of beds, and socialize only with the people of the host culture. You will even take up citizenship in the host country. You will renounce all homeland social security and insurance policies on your future, especially if the average citizen of your host country does not have these privileges.

Honestly, very few people from economically advanced countries can truly go native. Going native involves much more than most sent-ones will be able to do. Not everyone can live like Mary Slessor. Her host people said she was different from them, because even she had to return to England to care for her health while they remained in Nigeria!

An African proverb expresses the conflict of going native: "It doesn't matter how many days a log floats in the river, it won't become a crocodile." You have come from another culture. You will probably be of another racial group. You carry a different belief system than the host culture.

Remember—you are different!

The conclusion is a matter of conscience. You must do what is right, in obedience to Scripture. There will be differences that cannot be ignored or denied, but you can be genuinely *you* in the host culture if you accept these differences as a part of your calling. You can remove some cultural barriers, and you can work with the differentness without accentuating it. However, you must neither completely divest yourself of the home culture, thereby causing suspicion, nor bring so much of the home culture with you that you seem superior or stand out. You have been called to "walk as He walked" (1 John 1:6). That is a call to a balanced walk, where self no longer dominates you but your genuine identity is Christ living in you (Gal. 2:20).

Chapter 2

The Crisis of Language

*Learn the language that shares heartfelt
convictions*

WHEN YOU TAKE THE good news to another culture, the language
you use to tell the Story will determine how people will respond.
Marshall McClewen, communicator and writer in the mid-twentieth
century, coined the phrase, "the medium is the message." He con-
tended that the way we communicate tells the story. Poor use of
language will as surely cause the downfall of your mission as correct
language will build its success. For this reason I am convinced that
the language makes the Message.

In the film *My Fair Lady*, Professor Henry Higgins tries to
convince the street girl, Eliza Doolittle, that the most important gift
society has received from God is the English language. His
conviction expresses the sentiment of every language group or
people: "Our language is from God." Although non-Anglophones
may not thank God for the English language, they will praise Him
for their native dialect, which, they feel, correctly expresses all that
is important. This is a heart conviction.

The language in which a person thinks and meditates is the
dialect that he will most comfortably use when speaking to his god.
Thus, proficiency in the mother tongue of the host culture is essential
to effectively proclaim the gospel. The purpose of this chapter is to
review the practical attitudes and practices that help you to learn the
language of the people among whom you must communicate the
Truth. The language of the heart is the language of the good news.

Language study is to be a life-changing process. Learning a new
way to talk usually causes a crisis. On the other hand, to *not* learn the
language of the heart may provoke an equally serious crisis of

misunderstanding. The decision you make in the face of this challenge is career-defining.

Robert Moffat Wins Hearts[1]

The Scottish missionary, Robert Moffat (1817-1870), began working with the Bechuana people of South Africa in 1819. He was determined to Christianize the people with "the Bible and the plough." He and his wife, Mary, set up house in the Kuruman region. The people were gracious and they appreciated Moffat's efforts to teach them better gardening habits, but they could not understand his spiritual message. In the early years of ministry, he depended on local people to translate his gospel presentations, which was always inadequate because they understood little of his English.

Finally, after a full term of frustration and little responsiveness, Moffat decided to learn the language. He isolated himself from Kuruman, moving to a distant village where he struggled with the grammar and syntax of the Bechuana language for eleven weeks. It was a formidable task. Moffat had no training in language learning, much less in language analysis, but he returned to Kuruman speaking the language. He persevered until he was preaching intelligibly in the heart language of the people he served.

Word began to spread that the white man could talk the Bechuana language. He was telling them spiritual truth in their native tongue, and people came from distant places to hear this Message. They would return home with the Truth in their hearts. Even chieftains came, asking Moffat to arbitrate their inter-tribal conflicts because of his knowledge of their language.

Robert Moffat served the Bechuana people for fifty-three years. During this period, the church was planted, the Bible was translated, and literacy programs developed in this region. Moffat had tried in his early years to take a language shortcut, but the results fell short of his expectations. When he began to speak the language of the people, his status changed, his influence increased, and the impact he made was eternal.

The Heart Language in the Bible

The Bible does not require missionaries to learn the host people's dialect, but there is a biblical rationale for learning their heart language. This understanding should give you courage and motivate you to pursue one of the most difficult tasks that you will face as a foreign worker. The purpose of this chapter is to demonstrate that the heart language of the host people is the language that will best communicate the gospel. This assumption is based on the reality that each of us comprehends a language that best expresses our deepest thoughts and most intimate feelings. That speech describes our character, personhood, and identity. It is this dialect that the Creator has implanted in the soul of every person.

1. God created people as the crowning glory of His work (Genesis 1:26–27; 2:19)

When God created Adam and Eve, He stated that their distinguishing mark was that they were made "in Our own image ... likeness" (1:26). The image of God is that element that differentiates humanity from other created beings. People are God-conscious worshiping beings, and God-conscious beings who are rational about their thinking processes. Keil and Delitzsch summarize this quality as "the spiritual personality of man, though not merely in unity of self-consciousness and self-determination ... a creaturely copy of the holiness and blessedness of the divine life."[2] Louis Berkhoff, a Reformed Church theologian, includes several qualities in the image of God:

> Original righteousness, or more specifically, true knowledge, righteousness, and holiness ... not a state of moral neutrality ... includes elements which belong to the natural constitution of man ... a rational and moral nature.[3]

The first created couple responded to God and His creation, and they communicated with one another in a manner not found in animals. God *instructed* the couple to multiply their own race and to subdue the earth, ruling over every living thing (1:28). In Genesis 2 "the Lord *commanded* the man ..." (2:16). Finally, He brought before His created representative all the animals and birds "to see what he would *call* them; and whatever the man *called* a living creature, that was its name" (2:19).

Our first parents clearly demonstrated a created quality that no animal possessed. As the Creator had commanded them, they gave names to every animal. Their ability to communicate intelligently and to distinguish the various animals through speech was the Creator's gift that set them above the rest of the created order. The ability to speak to others is unique to humans, and it is so deeply ingrained in humanity that we cannot be correctly described without it. We are born with a desire and need to communicate intelligently because that is the way God has made us.

2. Human language is a unifying force (Gen. 11:1-19)

"Now the whole earth used the same language and the same words" (v. 1). Keil and Delitzsch clarify the literal sense to be that there "was one lip and one kind of words."[4] This unity of language came from one original couple and it was again established through the line of Noah.

In Genesis 11, what distinguished humankind as being above the rest of the created order becomes the cause for their disobedience to God in whose image they were created. They conferred together to build a tower that would reach into heaven, thus enhancing their reputation and insuring that they not "be scattered abroad over the face of the whole earth" (v. 4). The unity of language gave them security. They had one identity, which they felt they must protect. The fear that pushed them to work together to maintain their name was the very cause for their not filling the earth (1:28) according to the order of the Lord.

The Lord commented that "they are one people, and they all have the same language" (11:6), and He knew that this unity of language would cause them to feel that "nothing ... will be impossible for them" (v. 6). To insure that people would not again use language as a tool to disobey His first order of filling the earth, God confused their language and scattered them (v. 9).

This confusing and scattering resulted in people distancing themselves from one another. Language became the dividing wedge that kept smaller groups together and distinct from other groups. Through language, Jehovah insured that humankind would fill the earth.

The emotional and intellectual nature of human words was the unifying feature after Noah. It gave power, self-esteem, and an identity. But it also went unchecked due to the spiritual indiscipline of the ancients, causing them to believe they could ultimately control their destiny. When God acted so "that one may not discern (understand) the lip (language) of the other,"[5] He touched the very core of personhood. As a result, people lost their security in themselves.

3. The birth of the Church is tied to heart language (Acts 2:1-12)

A hundred and twenty followers of the departed Jesus were praying together in a large room on the day of Pentecost when a noise from heaven like a violent, rushing wind filled the house. The believers were filled with the Holy Spirit and began "to speak with other tongues [*glossais*] as the Spirit gave them utterance" (v. 4).

The meeting that had been somewhat secretive suddenly became public. Jews who had come to Jerusalem from all over the known world for a special feast were native speakers of many different languages. Hearing the sound, they were drawn to the building where the disciples were praying. They "were bewildered, because they [the crowd] were each one hearing them [the disciples] speak in his own language [*dialekto*]" (v. 6). This strange but marvelous sound caused the visitors to ask how the Galileans could speak so many different dialects (v. 8) so that all of them could hear and understand the Message in their own language (*glossais*) (v. 11). Some thought that the believers were drunk, but Peter began to preach to the crowd in the common language of Jerusalem. This preaching, which the visitors also understood, brought them to the point of decision. They asked the apostles, "Brethren, what shall we do?" (v. 37). The words spoken in the common language convinced them of their need to change.

This is reminiscent of Paul's statement in which he affirms that, "tongues are for a sign ... to unbelievers" (1 Cor. 14:22). Paul goes on to point out that when the unsaved hear believers speaking in strange tongues, they will think that the believers are mad (v. 23). On the other hand, if an unbeliever hears a clear declaration of the Truth in the language he normally speaks, the secrets of the heart are disclosed, "and so he will fall on his face and worship God" (v. 25).

Paul's emphasis was not on whether these *glossais* are a heavenly or earthly language, but that whatever language is used must bring people to an intellectual understanding of their position before God. It must lead them to submission to the Savior. Paul therefore stated that in a service, "I speak five words with my mind, that I may instruct others also, rather than ten thousand words in a tongue [*glossai*]" (14:19).

When the proclamation of the gospel is done in the language that is best understood by the people, there will be a far greater interest and a more intense response. Whatever dialect is used, it must be understood by the hearer so that his or her heart can open to Truth.

In summary, God speaks to each people group in their heart language. The language used is the verbal expression of the heart and the identifying mark of the individual. Personhood and dignity are wrapped in the language that each one has learned from their parents. That ability to communicate and express thoughts, emotions, opinions, and needs comes from the Creator. It was originally declared "good" and was to be used in a way that distinguished humankind from the animal world, but sin affected human identity in language. Nevertheless, God has given us hope that this divisive element will finally be overcome. We have a foretaste of that thrill of unity whenever people of different nations come together to worship Jesus. This anticipates the wonderful sounds that all of God's people will express in the future worship before His throne (Rev. 7:9).

As a sent-one, you face the crisis of finding the best way to overcome the language barrier. Only when you have crossed the barrier can you tell the Story so as to touch the heart of the receptor. The hearer will receive it more freely because the Message is on his or her psycho-linguistic turf. This is why you must step out of your comfort zone in order to reach the host people by speaking in the language of their heart.

Speak the Best Language for the Message

The language of the receptor's heart is the language in which the gospel will be most easily understood. Today's changing world, however, confronts some foreign workers with several choices. Often you will discover in the same country the existence of a heart language and a trade language—the commercial or secondary education language that nearly everyone speaks. Although the country may have dozens of ethnic groups, each one having its dialect, there are people in all these ethnic groups who also speak the commercial language. This secondary language presents you with the option of sharing Christ in a language that may not be of the heart. When you must choose between the government language and the heart language, you could ask yourself, "Should I use a secondary language that more people understand, or should I learn the ethnic dialect that only one group understands?"

The trade language may be easier to speak, and it may make you more mobile, but you should evaluate four important challenges of the trade language before making a decision.

1. Ministry may begin quickly, but effectiveness will be limited

The trade language often provides more adequate learning materials. High schools or universities back home might provide courses in this language, enabling you to begin study before leaving for the host country. The language might be more quickly learned. Upon arrival, you can immediately begin communicating with people because you speak the same language. It is possible that in your self-imposed urgency to get the gospel out before the Second Coming, you will be tempted to use the easy-to-learn language.

Let us look at some heart factors. What is the history of the trade or educational language of the host culture? French and English, for instance, were the imposed languages of the colonial era in much of Africa and parts of Asia. Today these are often associated with a history of oppression and foreign control. For some people, the language brings up memories of mistreatment and loss of personhood and dignity. Or the use of these languages is tied to commerce and trade, which could also give a wrong connotation to the Message.

Then there are trade languages that are not associated with colonization. For example, a tribal language might have become the language of the government through military might. For example, Congo uses forms of Lingala, raising memories of the oppression of Mobutu's regime. In parts of West Africa, Mandingo or Maninka are trade languages passed down by the invasion of Islam through the

Bambara and Manding races. In Latin America, Spanish and its variant forms arrived with the conquistadors. This situation has repeated itself in many nations around the world, creating an aura of oppression for the tribal people who do not speak the official language in their homes.

The point is that if your listener's past religious experience is in the language closest to the heart, what will be his gut reaction when he hears religious information in his oppressor's language? Will he really accept the new information, or will he have subconscious fears that this, too, will oppress? As Jacob Loewen rightly notes, "Because the trade language is not the language of a person's heart and of past religious experience, it may affect his receptivity ... or limit the depth of its penetration into the inner life."[6] Using the trade language may insert you into ministry more quickly, but it may also complicate the process of gaining of followers for Christ.

2. The educated class may come to Christ quickly, but the commitment may be shallow

People who have completed high school or university, or those involved in commerce requiring fluency in the secondary language, may be more easily reached with the trade language. They have become more accustomed to using it and therefore, their subconscious resistance to the trade language is lower. But let us again consider some heart factors.

First, what language does this person with whom you share the gospel use to communicate with his or her spouse? In the intimate moments with family members, those moments when people react quickly, do they use the trade language? When a person is involved in her native religion, whether formalized or traditional, does she use the trade language?

Second, students and intellectuals who have former religious commitments may prefer the trade language to talk religion as a way of keeping the Truth distant from their own heart. This keeps religion at the intellectual level. As a result, when someone does make a commitment, it may not be of the heart. Loewen points out that this convert may acquire a very superficial (if not warped) understanding of the Message. His trade or educational language may limit his religious experience to that vocabulary and context, again keeping it from a deep heart commitment.[7] A religious commitment in the foreigner's language insures that the religious experience remains foreign.

3. The trade language allows you to serve greater numbers, but it may limit intimacy in relationships

The trade language is known by a large number of people. If you know and use the trade language for ministry, you will be able to work with all the ethnic groups who speak it. This appears to increase your long-term influence in the country, but there is a down side to this broadened impact: you will limit your understanding of the host culture, because the trade language is a second language.

Language learning is a cultural learning experience. As you struggle to understand how people communicate, you will also learn how they think and why they see life the way they do. You will learn how relationships and family structures operate. Although you are an outsider, through the heart language, you slowly become an insider. The heart language is the primary mark showing that a person is an insider or "one of us." A host people will forgive most of your foreign eccentricities if you speak their language.

Many will have the experience of riding in a bus or train in which the locals are speaking in their common mother tongue, thinking that you, the foreigner, do not understand. You may feel self-conscious, especially when they comment on your appearance or clothing, but as soon as you respond to them in their heart language, the barrier falls and they remark about how you are "one of us because you talk like us!" The trade language keeps the outsider a step away from intimacy, whereas the heart language opens the door to people's heart.

4. Use the language that will best contextualize the gospel Message

This challenge surfaces as you struggle to choose between the trade language and the mother tongue or vernacular. In preparation for cross-cultural work, you probably learned the theory about contextualizing your ministry for the host culture. You came to the host people with theories and methods that you believed would adapt the gospel to them, but your single greatest contextualizing act will be that of communicating the Story in the mother tongue. David Hesselgrave clarifies this:

> Success in our missionary task means we *must* communicate the true nature of the world's danger and the divine provision for salvation, and we *must* attempt to persuade men to take the proper steps to save themselves and others. How does one do that apart from language? ... If one wants to communicate Christ to a people, he must know them. The key to that knowledge has been, and always will be, language....[8]

How many missionaries have gone through their career and looked back with regret that they didn't do better in learning and using the language? Some veteran missionaries promise themselves, "I really should brush up on that language." Unfortunately, it is too late. Ministry demands are already too many to allow them to take time out to study. They may persevere, but they may do so struggling with jealousy and anger toward those that are having greater fulfillment in ministry because they speak the language of the heart.

Conquer the Language Crisis

The biggest hindrance to language acquisition is attitude. Conversely, the greatest stimulant to language fluency is also attitude. The following are eight steps that will help you to attain and maintain the right attitude for conquering the language crisis.

1. Be a realist

Very few people have whizzed through language learning. It is tough. The average length of two years that it will take to learn the language will be the most difficult period of your life. But as you struggle with the difficulties, remember that there are thousands who speak this language fluently. You learned one language in your childhood too! It is also possible for you to speak this one. You aren't likely to get the gift of tongues in this language. Be prepared to work, pray, cry, be embarrassed, laugh, and rejoice. It is tough, but fluency is possible. Some people may receive from the Holy Spirit a "gift of languages" that enables them to more quickly acquire the words. Others have a greater aptitude for learning languages due to childhood exposure to multiple dialects. Still others, who specialize in language learning and translation, have learned the techniques that make this process seem like a game.

In the final analysis, if God calls you to cross-cultural ministry, He will enable you with what is needed to learn the host language. If you have grown up with limited exposure to other languages, be comforted in the knowledge that this is a process that many before have accomplished by the power of the Spirit of God. The greatest enhancement to your learning is attitude. This motivates you to get out and learn the language with the people, while your self-discipline in study speeds up the process.

2. Learn to listen

Discipline yourself to listen for comprehension. Teach your ears to hear the language in its context and with its own images. Learn to listen for specific grammatical forms of the language. During your study, choose the types of phrase forms you will need to learn for each lesson. Be attentive when you are visiting people and working with a native speaker. The language-learning guide in the appendix outlines those grammatical forms in a checklist.

International Linguistics in Kansas City, Missouri, publishes four booklets of action and story pictures called *Learnables*.[9] These are excellent aids to help the language student listen for comprehension. They contain only pictures (no printed words) that tell a story. The first volume begins with elementary sentence structures that are needed for survival, and the subsequent volumes progress to more complex language forms as your comprehension increases.

3. Learn to speak

One must speak the language to communicate the gospel. Most language courses provided in universities and high schools are designed to help analyze the language, making it an academic exercise. You should focus on learning to *speak* the language. There will be intellectual struggles when learning the grammar and vocabulary, but you are learning those rules and forms so you can correctly speak the language with others. This means that you will need to develop relationships with native speakers so you can practice on a regular basis.

For some people, speaking may be more formidable than listening. You may be so anxious about developing relationships with strangers that your mouth locks shut! Or you may hesitate to experiment with new words because you fear rejection. Soon you find many good reasons to stay in your comfortable home where you are at least accepted. But the problem with this is that you are not learning to converse with people who habitually speak the language. If this is your fear, you are in a comfort-zone dilemma. Each of us has a comfort zone where we know we are accepted and belong. Some of us are more fearful of the rejection that could come from stepping out of our comfort zone. If this is your fear, perhaps it would be helpful to do a personal research of writings that will lead you to self-evaluate. Ask the Holy Spirit to show you the steps you can take to overcome this anxiety.

Prevent comfort-zone fear. Make it a goal to develop one new cross-cultural friend each week until you have five dependable relationships. Then deepen these friendships into language-learning comfort zones, in which you can use your new words and get the encouragement and feedback you need. Remember speaking comes as a result of listening. Anxiety to speak should not overcome the all-important step of being a listener and an imitator of the sounds and forms. You must find ways to verbally express the host language. This is the reason for which you have come.

4. Get help from the experts

Many languages have written materials or language-learning aids. Check the national university and national literacy programs. Research other mission organizations, especially the Roman Catholic ministries (if they preceded you). If you have no pre-existing language-learning helps, seek some short-term technical training in language reduction and analysis. Avoid the error of reinventing the wheel, especially if others have already put the language in writing.

5. Develop a measurable plan

You will need to have personal assurance that this week you learned something new. Your goal is to be able to say at the end of each week, "I made progress!" To do this you must have a step-by-step plan that shows your progress. Even in times of depression and doubt, you need to be able to look at your plan and see that you are still on course. Appendix A gives a helpful and flexible checklist of measurable steps that will help you through an informal language program. Consult the reading list for other helps.

6. Concentrate on one project until you are successful

You have your steps laid out. You know your priorities. Stick with them and don't allow other ministry invitations to take you away for extended periods. In the struggle to progress, you will cry out for a feeling of ministry fulfillment. You will fight loneliness and the desire to be included and feel important. That desire will one day be fulfilled but first, concentrate on the task at hand. Focus on each week's goal and rejoice with local friends when you have climbed each small slope of the mountain.

7. Interruptions are for mind rest

Expect that there will be events, programs, and emergencies that take your time away from your plan. This does not contradict the principle mentioned in the previous step. It is a fact of life. The children will get sick. A water pipe will burst. The local market will not have kerosene when you need it. There will be a death in the community that needs your sympathetic presence. These are all opportunities to give the brain a momentary breather, allowing the mind time to assimilate and consolidate its forces. Much intellectual fuel is burned in language learning and some interruptions can give the motor a rest. But don't let the interruptions be excuses to lose focus. Use them to learn how to speak. If your child is hospitalized, use what you know of the language, even if the doctor thinks you are crazy. If the electricity fails, contact the electrician and speak to him in the language. Just don't touch any wires! If the tire goes flat, take it to the mechanic who speaks the language you are learning. He will help you with the vocabulary because his income depends on it.

8. Develop relationships with native speakers

Use friendship bridges to reach the goal of your study—speaking. Continue to develop relationships with people in the community who speak the language. This cannot be done adequately with a domestic helper with whom you have an employer-employee relationship, but a neighbor who just wants to be your friend will listen and respond. Most non-Western non-industrialized countries are relationship focused, so step out of your house and your comfort zone and go meet native speakers of the language! It is the best way to learn.

Saved by the Heart Language

A foreign worker was driving through his neighborhood when a teenager on a motorcycle came from a side street and crashed into his vehicle. By the time the worker got out of the car, a large crowd had gathered around the boy. Some young men, who had appeared for the occasion, were heatedly discussing in their local dialect how they could get money from this foreigner because of the accident. The sent-one only listened. As the discussion built to an emotional crescendo, some ladies sitting nearby selling oranges came to the men.

"You can't get any money from him," they declared. "He is one of us! He talks our language!"

With this introduction the stranger greeted them in their heart language. The discussion stopped and some walked away in shame. The sent-one was able to quietly settle the problem with the boy's parents, who also lived in the community. That night, the "alien" family went to sleep thanking God that they had gone through the trouble of learning the heart language of the people among whom they ministered.

Chapter 3

The Crisis of the Social Gospel

Give help that does not hinder the Message

HOW MANY TIMES HAVE you explained the Story to someone thinking that the Message was the reason why he was not interested? So you may have thought that you should change the Message. Perhaps the problem wasn't the Message. It is possible that the listener had another more apparent need that was blocking them from hearing and responding to the gospel.

For most of the twentieth century the evangelical church has endured repeated conflicts over Christian practice and theology. One of these battles centered on the social gospel. Evangelicals have tried to balance the demonstration of compassion for physical need with the declaration of the gospel. Yet some, out of fear of being condemned by their colleagues, created an imbalance whereby there was either very little compassion and too much declaration, or large doses of compassion devoid of the Message. Most foreign workers learn early in ministry that declaration through demonstration is a must. They recognize that there will be little or no response to the gospel Message when the listener is hurting. Sent-ones of this generation have their own way of soliciting funds that enable them to lend a helping hand as they share the Truth.

The purpose of this chapter is to provide guidelines that lead to a holistic way of giving help that does not hurt. Principles will be presented that will help you to discern ways to maintain a balance between declaration and demonstration.[1]

John Paton's Well

The Scottish missionary, John Paton, served for nine years on the Pacific island of Tanna (1858–1867), among a people who were savage and deeply entrenched in traditional religion. The fear of evil spirits, curses, and ancestors occupied their thoughts. Paton had confronted these occult powers by eating hexed fruit, proving the superiority of Jesus' name, and even the shamans admitted that Jehovah was more powerful. Yet, in spite of the gospel presentations, very few people committed themselves to Jesus. When intertribal conflict posed a threat to their lives, Paton and his colleagues were evacuated to the neighboring island of Aniwa.

The people of Aniwa were friendly, but only because they wanted the material goods that the white man brought them. Having lived for centuries on an island without fresh water, they had learned to gather rainwater in cisterns, and rationed their supply until the next storm came off the sea. As a result, water-borne diseases were common. John Paton felt he must dig a well in order to prevent illness, but the island chief would not accept John's proposal to dig down for water when, according to him, "everyone knows that water only comes from the sky." Despite the opposition, Paton persisted and began to sink a well near his house. His colleagues from a nearby island helped dig through hard volcanic rock. As he worked with pick and shovel, the chief would mock him saying that their Missi (the local word for the missionary) had gone mad.

The work continued until, at a depth of thirty-two feet, Paton stood in clean fresh water. The chief looked at this miracle and rallied his villagers to help. They organized themselves into teams and built the rock wall in the well shaft. Paton taught them how to lower the pail down the shaft and draw up water.

Once the well was assured, the chief, who was still not a follower of Jesus, came to Paton and asked, "Next Sabbath, will you let me preach a sermon on the well?"

The missionary was surprised but pleased and replied, "If you will bring all the people with you."

The next Sunday morning Chief Namakei began his sermon in front of his villagers, emphasizing his conviction and punctuating his phrases with his tomahawk:

Since Missi came here, he has talked many strange things we could not understand ... we thought the strangest idea was about sinking down through the earth to get rain! ... But the Missi prayed and worked on, telling us that Jehovah God heard and saw, and that his God would give him rain. Was he mad? Has he not gotten the rain from deep down in the earth? We mocked at him; but the water was there all the same.... From this day I believe that all he tells us about his Jehovah God is true.... No god of Aniwa ever answered prayers as the Missi's God has done.... Something here in my heart tells me that the Jehovah God does exist.... Henceforth, I am a follower of Jehovah God.[2]

John Paton's well sparked a people movement to Christ that was the turning point of the spiritual awakening in the South Sea Islands. Belief came because the people saw the power of God in the creation of a well. Paton had not planned it this way. No theologian convinced him of the dangers in confusing social demands with preaching. Nobody was there to argue about the virtues of "gospel only" as opposed to "welfare and social justice." He simply met the urgent need for a clean glass of drinking water. Quenched thirst became the voice that opened the people's heart to Christ.

The Primitive Church: Good News for the Soul and the Body

Jesus declared His purpose for ministry during His first teaching appearance in Nazareth. He spoke to the people in the synagogue using the prophet Isaiah as His text:

The Spirit of the Lord is upon Me, because He has anointed Me to preach the gospel to the poor. He has sent Me to proclaim release for the captives, and recovery of sight to the blind, to set free those who are downtrodden, to proclaim the favorable year of the Lord's (Luke 4:18–19).

Jesus outlined His ministry as being anointed by the Spirit of God to announce the gospel and meet the physical-social needs of the people. He did not separate them into two ministries but, quoting the prophet Isaiah (Is. 61:1–2), showed that His ministry was one Message of the good news of God's Kingdom. This kingdom would be ushered in by means of a Spirit-empowered encounter through the spoken word and the visible manifestation of God's presence.

There are many examples of the holistic ministry of Jesus. He healed the paralytic who had been lowered through the roof into His presence, fulfilling His previous statement, "Friend, your sins are forgiven you" (Luke 5:20). He delivered the demonized man who returned to his people and told them that he no longer lived the insane cemetery life, thanks to Jesus (Luke 8:26–39). Jesus dined with Zacchaeus, the corrupt tax collector who gave up his life of cheating, repaid his enemies, and become a follower of the Son of Man (Luke 19:1–10). Jesus used these events to teach the disciples that human problems are profoundly rooted in an original sinful nature. He touched a physical or emotional need in order to reach deeper into that human condition, thereby healing the soul that was separated from the Heavenly Father. Jesus showed that the problems of disease, infirmity, evil spirits, and Pharisaic legalism were only symptoms of a deeper separation. By addressing the immediate felt need, He enabled people to recognize the more pressing inner sin. Throughout His earthly ministry, Jesus balanced the two without creating a dichotomy in His theology of doing mission.

The New Testament church, beginning at Pentecost, proclaimed the same good news of the Kingdom with the same impact. They did not dichotomize social action and declaration. Rather, the two worked together to convince onlookers that these followers were indeed "Christians" [literally *little Christs*]. The apostles Peter and John wanted to help the lame man at the temple, but they had no money. So they simply declared, "In the name of Jesus Christ the Nazarene, walk!" (Acts 3:6). It is no accident that the writer of the Book of Acts quotes Peter as calling Him "Jesus of Nazareth," connecting this miracle to Luke's introduction in the gospel account (Luke 4:18–19). What Peter did at the Temple gate was in keeping with the mandate of Jesus to His "Christ-ones." Later, the early believers shared everything they had (Acts 4:32), forming a social community that impacted the needs of the followers of Jesus. Is it any wonder that the next verse states that "with great power the apostles were giving witness ..." (v. 33)?

Many examples describe how the apostles healed the sick, delivered the demonized, took care of the widows and orphans, buried the dead, and shared money with the hungry, all "in the Name." This was performed with the intent of preaching repentance and the forgiveness of sins through Jesus. Dr. Gordon Wetmore, in his paper presented to the Association of Evangelical Relief and Development Organizations, presents three findings from his study of the Book of Acts:

1. The ministries of the *Book of the Acts of the Apostles* are a continuation of Jesus' ministries as described in the *Gospel of Luke.*

2. The assumption that ministry to human temporal need is the responsibility of the community of Christian faith is found repeatedly throughout the book.

3. There is a dynamic combustion that occurs when this social ministry takes place in symbiotic combination with anointed preaching and teaching of the gospel.[3]

Holistic ministry of the local church was normal for the church as the Body of Christ. The believers associated themselves with the problem-solving ministry that brought about a change in their society and transformed hearts in Jesus' name. They interwove declaration with demonstration of compassion. John Stott describes this principle of balance:

Social action is a partner of evangelism. As partners the two belong to each other and yet are independent of each other. Each stands on its own feet in its own right alongside the other. Neither is a means to the other, or even a manifestation of the other. For each is an end in itself.[4]

Mission history shows that this pattern has continued throughout the ages. Christians have established hospices for the sick and dying, and they have built hospitals and trained nurses. They have stopped disease, opened orphanages, ended religious prostitution, halted the binding of women's feet, weakened caste systems, slowed polygamy, enhanced women's rights, stopped the murder of twins, terminated the sacrifice of widows, increased harvests, reformed prisons, and transformed lives by interweaving the declaration and the demonstration of the gospel through the power of the Holy Spirit.

Touch the Soul—Give Help that Helps

The twentieth century has proven to be unpredictable for the expanding Message of Truth. Countries that once were bastions of Christian faith became atheistic and violently opposed to the name of Jesus. Peoples that had received the earliest gospel witness told missionaries to go home. Freedom of religious expression was clamped by the restrictions of the secret police. A visa that had been given for "Christian missionary activity" was suddenly revoked for that very reason. Being a religious worker or church planter was no longer an acceptable vocation in some countries. At the dawn of the twenty-first century, the sent-one must be able to contribute to society if he wants to enter and live in the host nation. Therefore, touching the soul and the body has become an approved entry point.

The point of tension, however, is that the helping hand can quickly be overcome by the crying physical need. As you offer help, you suddenly realize that there are more demands and deeper needs. You are overwhelmed to the point that you burn out emotionally, if not financially. How can you manage the crisis of balancing help for the body and healing for the soul? Allow me to propose nine principles that will lead a worker or a church planting team to merge declaration with demonstration, so that you provide help that does not hurt. These suggestions presuppose that one is working in a culture in the stages of economic development rather than in a financially stable country.

1. Understand why you want to help

People from wealthy countries usually arrive in their adopted land with a clear memory of the good life back home. You, too, may have been accustomed to an easy lifestyle that the two-thirds world may only experience in dreams. As a "have" you may quickly feel guilty that you possess so much whereas others "have not!" You feel shame, guilt, and internal conflict because of all that you see. The crippled beggar reminds you of a brother who was healed through orthopedic intervention. The child digging through your garbage for some meat reminds you of all the junk carried away by City Disposal back home. The local pastor who can't afford school fees for his children reminds you of free public education in your country. For the first time perhaps, you feel guilty about the hurting people and want to relieve your pain.

You can relieve some of this pressure if you would work through a pre-action study. This can be done any time you or your team is facing the question about initiating a social project. This process will help everyone involved to evaluate why they want to give help. Use the following questions as a springboard for self-analysis. Write down the answers to each item measuring its biblical validity, its correspondence to your mission statement, and its application to the host people.

A. What is causing you to feel this way? Describe the circumstance that initiated the desire to act. Describe the feelings that surged inside as you saw this need.

B. Does meeting this need help fulfill your mission statement? If yes, how? If no, is a negative answer a legitimate reason to reject the need?

C. How long can you help with this need? It may be that once funds run out, stopping the help will create more harm than not responding to it.

D. How will the name of Jesus be enhanced? How will assistance affect the people's understanding of the meaning of the gospel? Will they want to come to Christ because it is a financial lift? Will they see salvation in Christ as de facto deliverance from a culturally determined class? How will this affect their understanding of repentance and conversion?

E. What other social ministries have already been tried in this setting? It helps to evaluate the history of social aid in the region. There may already be similar programs that have been or are being provided by non-governmental organizations (NGOs). If so, will a faith-based project be effective or needed if it has the same objectives as the NGO? Did the previous projects succeed? Why or why not? Answering these questions will enable your team to discern the local worldview's response to help and guide you away from past mistakes.

F. What detriment or asset will the action cause to the community's self-esteem? Will it empower them to advance on their own, or will it become another proof that they are incapable of helping them in the absence of the wealthy foreigner? Will this further hinder the community from seeking its own solutions?

G. What precedent is being set? What expectations are being raised by the action? What lesson are you demonstrating about empowerment and its influence on the Message? What conclusions about your spiritual values and the values of the gospel will your solution teach?

H. What kinds of words will be used to publicize this to your support network back home? The terms you use and the manner of presentation will tell whether you are colonizing, building your kingdom, and using people to enhance your position, or truly "planting the seed and watering the soil that God might bring the increase" (1 Cor. 3:7).

I. Where will you find the knowledge resources to properly meet the felt need? Just because you feel compassion for the felt need does not guarantee that you understand how to address that need. A poorly done job can have a more negative impact than doing nothing at all.

These are only a few of the questions that will help you to evaluate personal motives. Once the process is complete, you and your team will have a clearer understanding of what should be done and how you can proceed.

2. Choose action that will fulfill your mission statement

Reviewing your mission statement will help you to cut out the non-essential activities of ministry. This is important, especially in a context where urgent needs tyrannize your time. Assistance, especially financial, may become a cumbersome duty demanding so much time that telling the Story loses its position. Roland Allen points out that financial help can become a hindrance to fulfilling the goal:

> The primary importance of missionary finance lies in the fact that financial arrangements very seriously affect the relations between the missionary and those whom he approaches. It is of comparatively small importance how the missionary is main-

tained: it is of comparatively small importance how the finances of the Church are organized: what is of supreme importance is how these arrangements, whatever they may be, affect the minds of the people, and so promote, or hinder, the spread of the gospel.[5]

3. Integrate the gospel presentation into all aspects of community service

Your mandate is to declare the good news to all nations. This clarifies that all you do, whether in addressing physical needs, meeting intellectual needs, or conducting other social ministries, must bring people to the point of encountering Christ. "The Spirit is upon Me to announce" must be your conscious and driving motive. The apostles wove together the proclamation ministry and the demonstration of love in the power of the Holy Spirit, who in turn, assured the effectiveness of the holistic testimony.

The separation of social ministry and spiritual ministry is mostly a European and Western worldview problem. The Western social mentality and cultural fear of full commitment to a personal Jesus causes many Westerners to put religion in one box and social issues in another. Yet in most of the two-thirds world, this dichotomy does not exist. Religion and social life are intertwined. One behaves out of what one believes. This interwoven worldview creates an expectation on the part of the host community that the foreign worker's help and spoken word are one. Roland Bunch correctly states that most non-Western cultures believe that there is a spiritual message in our actions.

In many cultures people feel very deeply that the material and spiritual sides of life are vitally intertwined, and that man achieves happiness or fulfillment only through the balanced dedication of both. To these people, the program of human betterment devoid of religious emphasis seems strangely incomplete.[6]

The hindrance that often overwhelms social ministries, especially in the two-thirds world, is that social work is so immense that all our energies are spent in meeting these needs while the spiritual needs are left untouched. As such, the social ministry becomes the tail that wags the dog. Finances are prioritized in keeping with the need because to decrease that commitment would create a strong grassroots reaction. People will appreciate your response to their needs but that alone will not enable them to know your Savior. If you do not present the gospel while meeting physical need, some cultures may misinterpret the Message as one devoid of God's presence.

Care and wisdom must work together to hold a balance in compassion and declaration so that the Message is heard and seen as Truth. Reflecting on his missionary experience in Korea during the war years, Arch Campbell attested that there was something of deeper significance that must happen in the sent-one's compassionate presentation of Jesus.

Sometimes we are told that the approach must be through social uplift, sometimes through agricultural improvement, sometimes by cultural exchange, sometimes by loving service. All these efforts have their values and their influences. But nearly forty years of close acquaintance with the Christians of Korea, ... have convinced me that the message that really grips the heart, ... is ... the same message that gripped the great heart of Paul. "He loved me, and gave Himself for me."[7]

4. Listen to the host community

The host people know their hurts better than the stranger. The local people may have lived with their problems for many more years than the newcomer. If we can sit with them, observe them, and stop talking long enough to hear them, we may discover some deep felt need that will open the door to the heart of the people. Too often, the missionary comes to the community with a predetermined need, or identifies a need through his particular cultural filter. The ultimate success of the gospel is hindered when he wants to fulfill his interpretation of a need rather than discovering the need of his hosts.

Listening, for example, has led some Mennonite mission teams to develop reconciliation and peacemakers' programs in war-torn countries such as Columbia.[8] As the people find their inner struggles from war being healed, they in turn are more open to hear the deeper truth of complete reconciliation and peace with God through Christ.

A young Belgian Christian volunteer learned the importance of listening when he chose to do his military duty as a social-service worker with a Christian community in the Democratic Republic of Congo. This young man came with a well-prepared plan for helping the self-sufficiency of the church through an egg-farming project whereby chickens would produce 1,000 eggs every day. On-site listening, however, revealed that there was not a large enough clientele to purchase those eggs. So he stuffed the project back into his suitcase and began listening. This led him to organize parish-level coffee co-ops, and manioc and corn flour production. These were things that the local people understood, but they needed help to make them profitable. This young worker's success was born out of listening.

5. Empower the community to help and change itself

Your activity should lead the people to find their own solutions. Often the foreigner's help is a hindrance to this goal. He believes that he can solve this problem—after all, look at his home country! Roland Bunch states that when help does not empower the community to solve its own problems, it does not "set the captive free."

> Development is occurring where people are gaining the self-confidence, motivation, character traits and knowledge needed to tackle and solve the problems they have *by actually tackling and solving those problems.*

> 1. *Giving things* to people and *doing things for* people cannot be called development.

> 2. The development process whereby people learn, grow, become organized, and serve each other, is much more important than the greener rice fields and fatter corn purses that result.[9]

In the face of foreign criticism, Dr. Albert Schweitzer empowered the African community to meet their need. The French journalist, Alain Peyrefitte, was troubled when he saw how the famous doctor maintained a hospital in simplicity and poverty, when a modern French-financed hospital was available a short distance down the road. Furthermore, Peyrefitte did not understand why there were so few French nationals serving in this medical ministry. Dr. Schweitzer gave a stinging response:

> "The Africans feel lost in white lacquered rooms, with a room-mate that belongs to another tribe; many forgetting to eat and drink, die. I give them a hospital that they would have built themselves, and that they prefer coming to, even from a long distance.... They find rooms here similar to their own.
>
> "My patients," he continued, "are grouped by tribe. They are surrounded by their wives, who take care of their meals, children, animals ... they feel at home, they take courage and are healed.... The French ... have their own ideas ... they don't learn from experience. Experience hinders them.... Individuals change. A people don't [sic] change easily.... I have not come to metamorphose the French, but to heal the sick...."[10]

Schweitzer recognized that change is only helpful when the people understand its value. He initiated solutions to health that were culturally meaningful, while still using medical science in the context. He perceived that healing is a total cultural experience, not just a scientific result of correctly applied medical laws.

6. Change only what the community is willing and able to maintain

Meeting a social need will usually require that the mentality or thought pattern change. Those who facilitate programs need to identify the cultural patterns that are to be changed so that the ministry will impact the community. The Christian Message is first about transformation of a person's heart, out of which the society is transformed. A successful program will alter some elements of the people's worldview and, as the Message is accepted, the transformation is completed. Often, however, the sent-one introduces a project, thinking that it will be so successful that the host leaders will fully adopt it. But when he leaves, the people return to their old ways! Their worldview is neither changed nor are their lives transformed. William van Geest of Touchstone Consulting clarifies this problem in his presentation for the Churches and Development Workshop.

> The *fact* of belief change needs to be distinguished from *how* it is addressed. A variety of criteria or cautions regarding the

acceptability of belief change have emerged in the development community to deal with this tension. These include respecting and maintaining continuity of traditional culture, general sustainability of the development effort, and the involvement of local leadership in the development process.[11]

The way that this principle is respected will impact the self-esteem of the people. An imported project can be appreciated for its financial contribution. However, if the population cannot maintain the project on their own, the resulting failure becomes proof that they are unable to take care of themselves. They point to the rusty machinery and deteriorating buildings and say, "Our people do not have the intelligence of the foreigner. Look what happens when we try!" This sort of failure can also cause the people to demean themselves, making them feel that they must depend on the outsider in order to compete in this world. Keeping development within their means of success will help to avoid this.

A newly appointed pastor respected this truth. On arrival, he presented himself to the elders explaining his desire to live with them and teach them. The people accepted him, although the elders were unwilling to give him a field to cultivate his rice. He was patient and chose to become acquainted with the people, while gently sharing the gospel. He later discovered an unused plot of land. The locals said, "Evil spirits keep ruining crops there." He asked the elders for the worthless land, which they gladly gave to him. He prayed over his land, claiming it for Jesus, and set about organizing the irrigation flow through the plot. He planted rice using the new method he had learned at the Bible School from which he had recently graduated, transplanting shoots of rice into the paddy instead of sowing the seed to the wind. As a result, he had less weeding to do and the plants produced a better harvest. When the elders saw that the "demonized plot" produced a good crop, they asked him to explain his method and his beliefs. The villagers listened, and subsequently, became followers of Christ. They also changed their farming habits.

7. KISS—Keep It Simple and Small

The expectations of the community are often focused on immediate felt need. If there could be relief in that area, there would be joy. Often the foreigner comes to the community seeing the need through the worldview of his own country. Back home, he sees life as developed and well organized so he thinks he can manage these problems—and future ones, too! It is important for those who come from the industrial world to set aside those techno-complex assumptions, and plan small steps of change. Meeting immediate and small felt needs will be a more manageable approach and will produce more enduring results.

Think of the host worldview as a puzzle composed of many intricate pieces. If you change too many pieces at one time, the puzzle is ruined. But you can change the bigger picture one piece at a time.

Keeping it small will also help insure that your team remains focused on the mission statement. This is particularly important if the mission's purpose is more evangelism than social help.

An example of the KISS principle occurred with missionaries in a drought-stricken area of Africa. As the dry spell endured, they encountered mothers whose children were dying of diarrhea. The sent-ones chose a two-pronged solution. The men taught local family leaders how to make a simple water filter made of sand and charcoal. When the families understood the benefit of filtered water to their health, they began making these filters on their own. The women taught the local mothers how to prepare a simple rehydration solution by mixing sugar and salt in a liter of filtered water. As mothers saw their children regain strength, they began to understand some life-saving cause-and-effect principles. Later, when the rains returned, the people were appreciative of the workers' counsel and they listened to their Message with interest.

8. The people must claim the solution as their own

The people who are being helped by a relief or a development project need to feel ownership of the project or change. They need to see it as belonging to them because it will meet their long-term need. "Partnership" implies that they are a part of planning, developing, and execution of the program. They need to become excited and enthusiastic about their contribution. Local people need to lead and make their decisions without the monopoly of outside experts. This process may take time. The more deeply local people are convinced that "this is ours," the longer it will endure, and the greater will be its cultural transformation. Therefore, a well-planned program will begin small so that leaders grow into it and become a part of the whole picture of sharing Christ through compassion. Local involvement, however, may mean that you will feel that progress is not fast enough. But in most of the two-thirds world, quickness of progress is a foreign industrial value.

9. Analyze the social-economic effect of your project on the community

Before creating lift for a pressing social need, understand its larger and long-term implications. Sometimes uplift in one region will result in oppression to another. For example, a government project was designed to help an agrarian people living near the desert in Africa. The project improved the irrigation of crops by damming the large river enabling the people to have a year's supply of water for the fields. After the dam was built and the dikes constructed, it was discovered that another ethnic group downstream was starving because they depended on the now dried river for their fish.

The cause-and-effect factors of social ministry must be assessed. Finding the appropriate solution requires thinking long-term. If a harvest is increased, is there a practical use for this increase, or will the bonus crop rot in the storeroom? Will the socio-economic success gobble up the Message? In other words, will the Message become a victim of success?

Demonstrating holistic Christian compassion is a requirement in cross-cultural ministry, even as it was for Jesus' ministry. The New Testament writers also address this issue. James reminds us that without action, our faith is invalid (James 2:17–19). John states that without compassion for felt needs, we are testifying to the fact that the love of God is not in us (1 John 3:16–18). Paul visualizes imbalanced compassion as a resounding cymbal (1 Cor. 13:1). Let's submit to the Holy Spirit's guidance that meets the world at their crossroad of hurt, and share the Message that is felt in human feeling.

Chapter 4

The Crisis of Telling the Story

Tell the heartfelt Story through relationships

WE LIVE IN A WORLD of fads. The Western civilizations have developed inbuilt systems to constantly improve their technique. This fosters a hunger for more efficient ways to tell the Story. Workers sent from these cultures reach their host country with an ingrained passion to seek the best and most effective method to share the gospel. Many sent-ones dream of starting a people movement. Although the motivation is good, the methods may prove to be weak. Therefore, we ask, "What is the best way to tell the Story?" This chapter will help you to assess the most effective means for communicating the greatest Story ever told.

Hans Egede Gains a Hearing in Greenland

In 1717, Hans Egede (1686-1758) left Norway with his wife, Gertrude, and their four children and sailed to Greenland as missionaries. They reached their destination four years later and found it very difficult to adapt to the local lifestyle. They became even more depressed when they discovered that the Eskimo language bore no similarity to Scandinavian languages, and Hans would struggle to communicate throughout his career in Greenland. But he tried, with his limited language, to lead the Eskimo people away from their animistic habits. The locals responded to Egedes' caring home visits, especially during the long winter months.

Finally, the Message broke through their dark world in 1730, when smallpox ravaged the country. Hans and his wife gave themselves to serving the sick. People came from distant villages to be treated, and each one received a place to lie down in Egedes' home. Through the Egedes' sacrificial love the people began to understand the Message. They told Hans, "You have been more kind to us than we have been to one another ... and in particular you have told us of God and how to become blessed, so that we may now die gladly, in expectation of a better life hereafter."[1] In the years that followed, Hans' son, Paul, and the Moravian missionary, Christian David, introduced many Eskimo people to Christ.

The Primitive Church Communicated Christ

A brief look at the New Testament church encourages us to seek the most effective way to communicate the gospel. The early believers spoke so much about Jesus and His resurrection that the ruling authorities were "greatly disturbed" (Acts 4:2). Even under threat, the disciples told their accusers, "we cannot stop speaking what we have seen and heard" (Acts 4:20). Their method was to talk person-to-person. A study of the words used by Luke in the book of Acts shows that the Order "you will be my witnesses" (1:8) was enacted in a variety of ways. In these diverse approaches, the Message was personal, relational, and verbal.

1. Witness

In Acts 1:8 and 10:39, the word *martureo* means to be a witness, to bear witness, to testify, that is, to affirm that one has seen or heard or experienced something. The messenger knows it because he was taught by divine revelation or inspiration.[2] The witness tells what he has experienced. It is something that is given away. The word "martyr" is rooted in this Greek term. So the disciples were willing to die for that truth. Luke recounts that they boldly gave testimony to what they had seen and heard. It is a personalized message that is totally dependant on the messenger's experience.

2. Proclaim

In Acts 13:5 the word *katangelo* means to openly proclaim, publish, or announce. Joseph Thayer states that, in some cases, it includes celebrating, commending, and openly praising. The word is ordinarily translated as "preach." We read that "when they reached Salamis, they began to proclaim the word of God in the synagogue" (13:5). This is the picture of an unashamed presentation of a message in front of a crowd. It connotes a one-way method of preaching with the audience responding only after hearing the message.

3. Teach

In Acts 13:12 and 18:11 the word *didasko* is used in the context of giving instruction, to transmit knowledge in an orderly and progressive manner. The new believers committed themselves to the apostles' teaching (Acts 2:42). Jesus told the disciples to "teach them to observe all that I commanded you" (Matt. 28:20). Teaching is most effective in an environment where the learners can interact with the teacher.

4. Evangelize

In Acts 14:7 and 16:10 the word *euangelidzo* is used to indicate that the good news is announced or proclaimed. It is "evangelized." Luke's term is translated in the NASV as "preach the gospel," which means to bring the good news. He who brings the good news is an evangelist. This pictures someone who comes with a message that gives the listener joy, relief, and peace. The Message is declared openly and joyfully, leading others to experience the same joy. In the cities of Lycaonia, Lystra, and Derbe, and the surrounding region, Paul and Barnabas "continued to preach the gospel," the *euangelidzomenoi* (14:7). After finishing in this region Paul received a vision inviting him to Macedonia, which led him to conclude that "God had called us to preach the gospel to them" (16:10).

5. Discuss

In Acts 17:2, 17 and 18:19 the word *dialegomai* is used when the interaction between two people becomes one of thinking different things, mingling thought with thought. It means to ponder or resolve in the mind, or to converse, argue, or discuss. The word draws a picture of a discussion where different ideas are exchanged for the purpose of understanding one another and coming to a conclusion, and can mean to discuss in view of changing someone's opinion. Paul went to the synagogue at Thessalonica for three Sabbaths and "reasoned with them from the Scriptures" (17:2). Later he "reasoned with the Jews and the God-fearing Gentiles, and in the market place every day" (17:17). When he returned to Ephesus, he "entered the synagogue and reasoned with the Jews" (18:19). He was selective in where and when he reasoned, limiting these encounters to people who already had a similar worldview and background.

6. Persuade

In Acts 13:43, 17:4, and 26:28 the word *peitho* is associated with *pistis* faith, meaning to induce one to believe by the use of words or to cause someone to believe in an idea. This is a verbal interaction that convinces the listener to accept the message. At Pisidian Antioch, after many discussions in the synagogue and with the Gentiles, Paul was "urging them to continue in the grace of God" (13:43). At Thessalonica "some of them were persuaded and joined Paul" (17:4). Here the people changed their belief and openly followed the new way. But persuasion did not always work. King Agrippa, after hearing Paul, replied, "In a short time you will persuade me to become a Christian" (26:28). In communicating the gospel, *peitho* demonstrates the strongest intent by the speaker to bring about change. The disciples did not fear persuasion. Rather, their eyewitness account was often so powerful that their words convinced the listener to change.

The Apostle Paul went to Athens to convince people about Christ (Acts 17:16–33). This was the first time that the gospel was presented to this city. Paul began by presenting the claims of the prophets to the Jewish people attending the synagogue. This proved difficult, and he later went into the city center to Mars Hill, where he found the philosophers and thinkers of the town who were ever ready for a debate. As Paul began to speak to them, they insisted that he come to the true place of debate, the Areopagus. Here he began his testimony by attracting their attention to a common point of the unknown God (v. 23). Paul continued his presentation by referring to their proverbs and poetry, using these transitional bridges to help them understand the gospel. Finally, he spoke about Jesus who was resurrected (v. 31). At this point, the crowd began to sneer at him. Others left. Some followed. A number said they wanted to hear more about it.

Some twentieth century interpreters accuse Paul of compromising his message at Athens, thereby diminishing the number of conversions. Yet Paul had come to a town that had received no pre-evangelism, as we know it. His presentation was their first hearing, and therefore, it *was* pre-evangelism. As a consequence, he did gain a small following as well as attract some who wanted to know more.

In summary, the apostles did not limit themselves to one style of verbal communication. They varied their approach in order to convince their audience. Careful study of each situation shows that each one was different and thus, required an adapted method of communication. Sometimes it was persuasion, debate, or reasoning; other times the apostles used teaching or preaching. But each situation demanded its own form of verbal communication and it is clear from all the settings that they used *person-to-person oral communication.* Relational evangelism was the priority.

Transfer the Story from Your Heart to the Listener's Heart

Let us look at six fundamental principles that are consistent in the apostles' method of communication. Understanding the passion and the practice of the apostles will guide us in choosing a method that best transfers the Message from our heart to the listener's heart.

1. Go to their turf

Every person in every culture lives in a safety zone, in which he feels more secure talking about his convictions. Think of how you depend on your comfort zone. You may feel frightened and tense when someone confronts you with new ideas outside of that area. You are more resistant to listening because you are not psychologically relaxed. Your listeners are not different. They may listen if you induce them to come to your ground, but their ears and hearts will be most receptive when you speak to them on their own territory. When they see you in their home, in their yard, or in their market, they know that you accept them. They will be more prone to listen when it can be done where they feel like they are in control. Some call this "finding common ground."

However, foreigners historically tend to congregate together in *their* comfort zones. In times past, the mission station was built and people were expected to *come* to the center church. The hospital and schools were all built in a central area for better management and efficiency. People were supposed to *come* to have their needs met.

Toward the end of the twentieth century, the development of the team philosophy in mission began to lead in the same direction. For example, building an activity center or an evangelism center placed the communication process at the same risk because it predetermined the place where people can *come to hear* the gospel. The New Testament pattern, however, always focused evangelistic relationships on the recipient's turf without bringing him or her to the church or Christian territory to listen.

Mission emphasis on big cities can also risk the same effect when workers prefer to set up house in the capital city or port city because the conveniences are available, schools accessible, and team members closer. These places also provide a quicker evacuation route during social unrest. Yet, when these amenities become a reason to not *go* into the communities to develop relationships with the host people, we are like the fisherman who throws the net in his bathtub. We really should be fishing where the fish swim. Better yet, we should be swimming with them!

2. Build relationships for sharing the gospel

The gospel is a message about a relationship with God that needs to be established. It is God's purpose to reconcile all things to Himself (Col. 1:20). Your Message is one that brings people together. So as the sent-one, seek to develop relationships that will bridge the Message into the heart of the host people. Live in their community and speak their language. Share in their emotional and cultural events such as birth celebrations, baby naming, funerals, weddings, and other festivities. These are all social events that establish common ground and become the emotional building blocks of security for sharing the Message. Seek opportunities for common events that build the experience-history that is the foundation on which trust is built. You will begin to put those building blocks in place when you have suffered with your people, when you have rejoiced with them and wept with them. This is what the Scriptures call us to do: "to rejoice with those who rejoice and weep with those weep" (Rom. 15:12).

3. Plant the seed abundantly

In Jesus' parable about the soils (Matt. 13:3ff), the farmer generously scattered the seed on different soils. The Lord's lesson is clear—kingdom people are seed-planting people. We must first plant the Message in peoples' hearts before they can become the harvest. The seed planted needs to be cultivated and watered, and in due time, God will bring the harvest (1 Cor. 3:5–9). Only when the harvest is ready does the reaper do his work.

Our industrial-world mentality battles the principle of sowing. We are culturally programmed to think in terms of the harvest, the quarterly report, and responsiveness of the audience. We want first to know if there will be marketable results, and whether the project is profitable. But Jesus wants us to be seed-planters who will allow Him to bring the harvest. Ignoring this simple guideline will result in a smaller harvest. As Paul, the master church planter wrote, "Whoever sows sparingly will reap sparingly" (2 Cor. 9:6). If you focus on planting only where there will be results, you will hinder generous planting. Furthermore, to plant sparingly may lead you to reap another person's harvest. As planters, our first duty is to develop the relationships that become heart-to-heart seed planting opportunities.

4. Use the most effective personal approach to make the Message understandable

The worker has been sent to communicate the Story of Jesus, which must be understood in the mind of the hearer. To do this, we must make four important commitments in communication.

A. Speak the language of the heart. The Message makes most sense in the language closest to one's heart. As you take time to learn this dialect you will also learn about the culture. The symbols that compose the language will become the pictures of communication. You will begin to understand the cultural meanings of the words that are not explained in the dictionary. Your spoken words will go from your heart to the heart of the receptor.

B. Describe biblical Truth in their cultural images and forms. Each culture owns its indigenous linguistic forms and pictures. These are found in the parables, proverbs, and stories that convey the values of the people. For instance, Hebrew culture used the stories of the Old Testament, the Proverbs of Solomon, and the songs of David. Cultures also have their extra-biblical traditions that can bridge Truth. For example, Western society has the stories of Hans Christian Anderson, Mother Goose, Aesop's fables, and many epigrammatic proverbs that are used to send a teaching value to its destination. Africa has its animal fables, and Asia has its cultural legends. Eastern Europe tells stories tied in with the Orthodox Church's cultural events, and France has the writings of its philosophers. Each culture also has its history and personal heroes. Learn these stories and proverbs in order to become an insider to the culture's thinking. They are like beams of light that penetrate into the heart.

C. Select the verbal approach that is appropriate to the situation and mentality. Learn to feel comfortable in a variety of oral communication styles. Dialogue may work well in an intellectual setting, but in another it may create a riot. Personal testimony may do well in a family setting, but is ignored on the street corner. Learn the Message well enough so you are free to use the appropriate verbal method for each new situation. Be flexible!

In Europe, for example, some think that there needs to be a highly philosophical approach. The ALPHA[3] study was developed by the Anglican Church to reach postmodern minds. Friends are invited to spend an evening in a small group to study important questions of life. Each lesson leads the participant closer to his or her spiritual need for the Savior. It is a highly relational and discussion-centered method that brings people to trust Christ in their comfort zone.

D. Share the Message without apology. The apostles did not compromise the Message. They renounced hidden ways (2 Cor. 4:2), always bringing the audience face to face with the claims of the death and resurrection of Jesus. There were times when this Story separated the crowd, causing many to turn away. But the eventual rejection of the Message did not cause the speaker to modify the content. The apostles always presented the true Truth.

Modern-day anthropology and psychology sometimes cause the Christian to be culturally or politically sensitive so as not to offend the listener. The emphasis on tolerance in pluralistic cultures causes people to fear the proclamation of the Truth. As a consequence, some Christians tend to hide the essentials of the gospel. Often they present a diluted Jesus who ceases to be "the Way and the Truth."

We must wisely present the gospel using verbal cultural bridges that are understandable and a language that is appealing, so that when we come to the true Truth, it will be understood as just that. The results need to remain in the hands of the Holy Spirit.

5. Model evangelism methods that the new believers can imitate

More spiritual truth is caught than taught. You teach more through your example than through your words. Always bear in mind that you are planting the church with a goal of seeing the new believers continue the work in their community. Remember also that these followers will try to imitate your evangelistic habits. Relational evangelism is the most transferable method of sharing the gospel. If you depend on hi-tech methods that they cannot support or reproduce, you have denied them the honor of telling the Story from their experience. They may opt out of a natural opportunity thinking that only the missionary can do evangelism because he has the equipment!

Literature is an excellent tool for evangelism in literate cultures, but if the host people are marginally literate and lack the internal financial structure for managing a full-scale literature ministry, then you shouldn't expect this work to continue with the same effectiveness. What the people cannot afford or manage, they will usually not imitate, although they may ask you or the sending agency to finance it.

This may be difficult for you to accept. You come from a society that "gets things done quickly and efficiently," and you may need some good statistics to write home about. You want the gospel to go to as many as possible as quickly as possible in order to "hasten Christ's return," but your methodology may say more about you than about the Message itself. Methods tend to be culture-bound or environment-controlled, but the simple Message can be understood anywhere, when told in an acceptable manner.

Humans are created to be relational beings and the gospel is about a relationship. The method Jesus gave for transmitting that message is a testimony that is relational. Relationships are transferable in any culture. Very few communication methods are as effective as verbal expression across the bridge of friendship. Mission history holds this truth as evidence.

6. Signs and wonders keep their appropriate position in the context

We read that "with great power the apostles were giving witness" (Acts 4:33) and that "many signs and wonders were taking place" (Acts 5:12). The Holy Spirit is able to demonstrate His power in order to validate the Message of Jesus and to announce to the world that the Message of the kingdom of God has arrived. These events are called "signs" because they point the recipient to the correct way, which is Jesus.

Always be prepared for the Holy Spirit to point the way, but the working of miracles and healing must never overshadow or replace the Message of Jesus' work for the world. People should not become Christians because they want a miracle. The life transformed by Jesus is already a miracle. People should come to repentance and conversion as a result of the outpouring of the Spirit.

Entering the Cambodian Heart

A young American couple named Jeff and Heather Williams moved to the Kampong Cham province of Cambodia in 1996 hoping to plant a church there. They rented a house and began making contacts in the community, but heavy rains and the worst flooding in twelve years soon dampened their intentions. Heather described their predicament as follows:

> Our neighborhood is completely under water.... [In] the road in front of our house the water is over my head.... We thank Him for the very high posts on which our house was built! We have more than three feet of water in the office downstairs.... We know many whose homes are flooded up to the roofs.

> The flood has brought all of us in our neighborhood closer together. We are working through the many difficulties of living

in an island of a hcuse.... It is a really unique way to bond quickly with our neighbors, who are doing the same thing![4]

Heather continued her story in a subsequent report:

At the time it [the flood] was annoying, but now we are thankful. Our neighbors kept asking when we were going to leave. When we told them we were not going anywhere, their curiosity was aroused.

The month that followed saw a steady stream of boats to and from our house, visiting here, talking there, taking food to those who had none, sitting dripping wet on neighbors' porches after swimming over to see how they were doing. Everyone was willing to listen, and everyone had loads of free time. When the water receded, one of the women asked us to teach the Bible in her house. Before too long, we started a second group. These people do not merely want to study the Bible; they want to devour it.[5]

Heather's story illustrates that when the Message is given a personal meaning, it penetrates the heart. There will always be results that lead to the planting the Truth in those hearts.

Chapter 5

The Crisis of Deciding for Christ

Lead seekers to embrace the Truth in a culturally-relevant manner

HOW MANY TIMES do you know that you are communicating the Message, but the listener makes no decision? You know you have told the Story. People nod or shake their head in assent and say, "That's good," but nothing further happens.

The human ability to make a decision came with the Creation. The first couple was given the ability to choose to obey God: "From any tree of the garden you may eat freely; but from the tree of the knowledge of good and evil you shall not eat ..." (Gen. 2:16–17). When Satan tempted Adam and Eve to eat from the tree, Jehovah did not intervene. He allowed them the freedom to make their decision.

Free and unforced decision-making is a quality of the image of God in humankind, but the freedom to make a decision is often violated. The evangelist is driven by the love of Christ to bring others to Christ. He may have traveled many days and through much danger to bring the Message to a new people. He may have crossed many cultures and overcome mountainous difficulties, just so he can share the joy of knowing Jesus. This makes it even more imperative that the listener decides for Christ. The temptation to *strongly* encourage a decision can become so overpowering that the evangelist will use less than dignified means to force a decision. When this is done, he has violated the God-given decision-making dignity.

The purpose of this chapter is to clarify how your listener makes a decision. My desire is that you will follow the cultural process of your listener that will lead him to decide for Christ.

Khalid's Neighbor Trusts the Messiah[1]

Khalid, who lives in a predominately Muslim country, grew up in an animistic family that served the sacrificial system of its ancestors. His people deeply hate Muslims, whom they perceive as invaders and thieves. Khalid heard the gospel through the testimony of an itinerant evangelist. The Truth of Jesus so transformed his life that all of his family members became followers of Jesus. He was not surprised to discover that the Christian community had the same dislike for Muslims as his animist friends. His parish and pastor were convinced that Muslims had already received their chance to follow Jesus but had blown it, so the door was now closed to them. This feeling often intensified in the Christian cell groups whenever tension mounted with the Muslim community.

When Khalid finished his university education, he was sent as a government worker to a town that is totally Muslim. There he became part of a small Christian group that also avoided their Muslim neighbors. Khalid learned from his personal Bible study, however, that "all have sinned" (Rom. 3:23) and that "whosoever calls on the Name shall be saved" (Rom. 10:13). He knew in his heart that this was also true for his neighbors, despite the attitude of his Christian brothers.

One day he heard the death wail from his neighbor's yard and he went to participate in the Muslim funeral. This opened the heart of Abdul, the head of the family, to Khalid and the two men began to meet regularly. As their encounters grew, Abdul asked questions about the Christian faith that Khalid was careful to answer in a way that the Muslim could understand. He asked Abdul to study the Bible with him, an invitation that was gladly accepted. Over the next two years, this Muslim man began to see that the Truth of Christ was real, that Isa really is the Messiah. He asked many questions about the meaning of conversion and its cost, and his friend patiently answered them. Khalid was anxious that a commitment be made, but he did not push Abdul. The day finally came when Abdul made the decision to place his trust in Isa. As he received forgiveness and the assurance of salvation, Abdul found a deep joy that he had not found in his former religion.

Over the next weeks, Khalid taught Abdul how to lead his family in prayer and Bible study. He showed his new brother the Christian way of obedience, always bringing him back to the Bible. Soon other family members made a decision to follow Isa. During the Ramadan fast, Khalid encouraged Abdul's family to fast for biblical reasons, as an act of faith and not out of religious obligation. Often, after a modest daily fast, Khalid would eat with Abdul's family, and his presence at the table stimulated some deep discussions about the Christian way of life.

Guidelines for Decision Making

There are seven guiding principles that will help you to evaluate the way you bring the seeker to the point of decision. These principles are not exhaustive in that they do not give all the background information for every culture, but they clarify the things you need to include in your ministry of persuasion.

1. The gospel must be heard

People need to hear something before they can decide to accept it. Jesus frequently concluded his parables with the remark, "He who has ears to hear, let him hear" (Matt. 11:15; 13:9; Mark 4:23), implying that hearing leads to obedience. He told the crowd, "My mother and My brothers are these who hear the word of God and do it" (Luke 8:21). The Apostle Paul reminded the Roman Christians that faith comes from hearing, "and hearing by the word of Christ" (Rom. 10:17). In the book of Revelation, John concludes in every letter to the seven churches with the injunction, "He who has an ear, let him hear what the Spirit says to the churches" (Rev. 2:7, 11, 17, 29; 3:6, 13, 22). The conviction of the biblical writers is clear, pointing us to three presuppositions about hearing and its correlation to decision making.

A. Hearing is essential to obedience. The listeners cannot make a correct decision if they have not first heard the gospel in their language. Just as one cannot obey something he has not been ordered to do, so too one cannot follow Christ without first hearing about Him and His expectations.

B. Someone needs to go and tell them so that they will hear. If hearing is important to making a decision, then it is imperative that they be told. They must hear the Message. People can only make a decision once another person has told them what they need to know. It is for this reason that Paul asked, "How shall they hear without a preacher?" (Rom. 10:14). This is why it is so important that you communicate in the language of your hearer. They need to understand the Message in their terms and meanings.

C. One who hears will choose to accept or reject the Message. In Jesus' parable about the wise and foolish builders, the foolish man heard and built his house on the sand anyway. Hearing itself was not sufficient (Matt. 7:26–27). There are those who will hear the warning of the watchman and will not act upon what they hear. Their destruction is on their own heads, because they did not respond correctly (Ez. 33:5). In the book of Acts, Phillip asked the Ethiopian eunuch, "Do you understand what you are reading?" The man responded with a question of his own: "How could I, unless someone guides me?" (8:30–31). This man had been listening to the guidance of the Holy Spirit. He came to Jerusalem seeking the answers that the religious people could not fully provide. Each step of understanding led him closer to the final decision into which Philip was able to lead him. The eunuch heard and, as a consequence, accepted the Message.

This principle requires us to know the mind and thought of the audience so that we will present the Truth in an appropriate way. But the Holy Spirit must also open the hearer's mind to understand the Truth in the proper cultural setting. The Message needs to pass through the cultural filtration system of the hearer and arrive in his mind as the pure Truth of the gospel. According to David Hesselgrave,

> Missionary communication must take into account the ways in which people think and formulate ideas.... The missionary can adapt because all people think postulationally, psychically, and concrete relationally. He must adapt because respondents of other cultures have their own priorities in thinking.[2]

Check the hearing process before pressing for a decision. Did the audience hear the Message well enough to understand its meaning? Can they respond to it?

2. The Holy Spirit must convince

You can inform someone of the Truth, but the Spirit of God must bring him to the point of decision. Jesus told the disciples that the Holy Spirit would convict the world concerning sin, righteousness, and judgment (John 16:8). When the Holy Spirit came on the day of Pentecost, Peter gave a clear biblical presentation of Jesus, the Messiah, to the crowd. It was the Holy Spirit who convicted the people of their sin (Acts 2:37), causing them to be pierced to the heart so that they asked Peter to show them what they must do.

The Holy Spirit must open the listener's understanding so that he will come to a decision. The disciples who talked with Jesus on the road to Emmaus realized, after they recognized Him, that His presence had affected their understanding. By His Spirit, Jesus was warming their hearts to the truth that they were hearing Him speak. In the days before His ascension, Jesus opened the minds of the disciples enabling them to "understand the Scriptures" (Luke 24:45). When Paul shared the gospel at Philippi, Lydia responded to the Message because the Lord had opened her heart to respond (Acts 16:14). Spiritual understanding comes as a result of a divine work in the hearer's mind.

Understand this principle apart from the need to hear and listen, because this is an act that only God can perform through the Spirit's persuasion. You want to persuade with a convincing presentation, but you may be tempted to press for results before the hearer is ready to decide. If you are assured in your belief that the Holy Spirit convinces people of sin, you will be less tempted to try to do it. John Stott clarifies this problem:

> We are all familiar with the development of modern psychological techniques in advertising ... in the deliberate inducement of mass hysteria.... But we Christians must make it clear beyond all doubt that evangelism is an entirely different kind of activity. We must refuse to try to bludgeon people into the kingdom of God. The very attempt is an insult to the dignity of human beings and a sinful usurpation of the prerogatives of the Holy Spirit.... For one inevitable result of evangelism by unlawful means is the leakage from the church of those whose conversion has thus been "engineered."[3]

Engineering a conversion is exactly what Paul was unwilling to do. He wanted his listeners to hear the Truth so that they could make a correct decision. He told the Corinthian church, "We have renounced the things hidden because of shame, not walking in craftiness or adulterating the word of God, but by the manifestation of the truth commending ourselves to every man's conscience in the sight of God" (2 Cor. 4:2). Follow the apostle's example and let the Holy Spirit do the convincing!

3. Lead people through little decisions until they make the most important choice

Every major decision is preceded by a series of minor decisions. Jesus always brought people through each step until they made the important decision. Many bowed in worship and submission (Luke 5:1–11), but some left Him (Luke 18:22–24). The apostles followed His example. At Pentecost the people came to a decision before Peter called for it (Acts 2:37). When the Samaritans heard the gospel presentation and saw the signs of Holy Spirit power, there was much rejoicing in that Samaria (Acts 8:8). The preaching activities of Paul brought people face to face with Christ and their need to decide for or against Him. Often there was a mixed reaction. Some believed and wanted more, whereas others scoffed in rejection. Still others wanted to think about it. In each case, they were brought to the point of deciding.

You need to bring the person to face a decision. It is helpful to keep in mind that the decision to trust Christ may not be the first decision a person will make in his spiritual pilgrimage. He has made a series of smaller choices before the decisive one. Consider the listener who has been raised in a culture and belief system that teaches that Jesus is not the Son of God. He must first move in the direction of acknowledging first the historicity of Jesus, then His person, then His deity. As the person is able to overcome smaller obstacles, you lead him through to the next decision, successively overcoming hindrances until he can fully grasp Christ.

James Engel describes the intellectual distance a person travels in order to decide for Christ. In his book, *How to Communicate the Gospel Effectively*, he illustrates a spiritual receptivity chart that positions a person according to his understanding of Christ.[4] One who has no knowledge of Christ may be located as much as -6 below zero, depending on the degree of his resistance and ignorance of Christ. As the non-believer makes decisions to listen and accept more Truth about Christ, he progresses up toward 0, which is the point of changing allegiance to Christ. After deciding to accept Christ's claims, he advances in receptivity to +1, +2, and beyond. In terms of personal evangelism, this graph helps to position the non-Christian on this scale in relationship to zero. The chart visualizes the smaller decisions that one must make before making the final decision to trust Christ.

A different explanation of this process is described in *The Seven Laws of Teaching*, in which John Gregory defines the step-by-step progression that leads a person to learn a new concept.[5] First is the stage of uncertainty or doubt. A person receiving new information will initially accept it with uncertainty because there is no place for this information in his mental filing system. He will evaluate it, usually with skepticism, referring to past experience and cultural reference systems that will prejudice his acceptance in positive or negative ways. If he allows the concept to continue in his thinking, the Truth will move to a second stage where he organizes the new concept in his mind and life, filing it where it is associated to something he already knows. If the person is unable to find this association point, his learning process will stop. When he finds the proper place for this information, he progresses to stage three, where he either accepts or rejects the new information.

These three stages are followed for every small decision that leads to greater or more important ones. For example, when someone who has lived all of his life in a culture controlled by a dominant formal religion, he will not be quick to accept the gospel at the first hearing. His background will have formed a grid in which he organizes the new thoughts. If this grid happens to have innate barriers to the gospel, he will probably reject the new Message. You cannot expect him to make a decision for Christ until he has had time to change the grid through which the new knowledge passes.

4. Present the gospel to social decision makers

Every society has its decision makers. They are those individuals in the community who are esteemed as the right people to make life-changing choices. Paul first presented the gospel to the people at the Synagogue who already had an understanding of the Old Testament and were the spiritual decision makers for the Jewish community. As a result, they were already closer (on the Engel's scale) to the point of accepting the Messiah. Once the Jewish leaders had decided, Paul moved to the larger community. When he witnessed to the jailor, he talked to a family head—a decision maker. In other encounters, the apostle asked to see the town's political leaders, anticipating the day when he would present the Truth of Jesus to the Emperor. Paul first sought the decision makers who could influence the thought and belief of the community, because they needed to know the new Message first in order to pave the way for others to listen.

Often a cold response to the gospel presentation may be the result of telling the Message to the wrong people. For example, a group of evangelists tried three times to bring the gospel to an unreached town in West Africa. Each time they used mass evangelism methods without first developing a relationship base, and each time they received a cool response from the adults, although receiving a warm one from the youth. Later, they became frustrated when the youth who had "converted" were no longer interested. The evangelists realized their error when a tailor, still a non-Christian, secretly told them what the old men were saying about the new religion. He suggested they befriend the elders first. The evangelists followed the tailor's advice and ultimately won entry into the hearts of the people.

Gordon Hedderly Smith, a missionary to Vietnam, describes how the reception of the gospel among the mountain people was much faster and enduring when he talked to the chieftain.

> This first trip to the north was by no means a loss, however. Many months later an old village chief gave his heart to the Lord, and it was not until some time after that he told us he had first heard the gospel at Buon Ho [a government center where Smith had presented the gospel to village chieftains alone]. He has since been baptized, with six others in his village.[6]

When decision makers choose to follow Christ, they open the door for all who trust them to follow. This creates group safety for new followers leading to what Donald McGavran calls a "web movement." In the *Bridges of God,* McGavran points out that in the two-thirds world, individuals are connected to families who are associated to other villages or towns. With this in mind, if a family head understands the gospel and responds positively, he will influence a host of relatives who respect him as the family father. In some societies, the family leader or village chief is considered the priest of the family who guards the souls of his clan. When his people see him make a decision for Christ, they will usually follow.

In many cultures, it is possible for a group to make a decision to follow Christ. Although each person may not understand the importance of the group decision, the fact that his people do it together creates the safety web in which individuals are discipled. McGavran states:

> Most people movements consist of a series of small groups coming to a decision.... A people movement results from the joint decision of a number of individuals—whether five or five hundred—which enables them to become Christians without social dislocation....[7]

He calls this a "multi-individual, mutually interdependent conversion."

Before you make too many plans for planting a church, it would be advisable to gain the approval of the decision makers.

5. Make a decision according to cultural decision-making assumptions

Understand how and why people make a decision. Jesus asked for decisions to be made by individuals and by groups. The apostles followed a variety of approaches, choosing what was relevant to the Greco-Roman world of their time. Some large groups made the decision (Acts 2), but other decisions were individually made (Acts 9). There were village decisions, as in Samaria (Acts 8), and there were family decisions (Acts 10). The apostles permitted people to make a decision to follow Jesus according to the Holy Spirit's leading and in keeping with the expectation of the group or individual. I believe that these converts persevered because they made a decision for Christ in a culturally meaningful manner.

Every culture has its decision-making assumptions. Certain cultures believe that the individual is free to decide as an adult while others believe that most individual decisions cannot be made without family consultation because life-changing decisions are to be made according to prescribed patterns.

People from Western cultures tend to overlook the importance of group decision making. Societies that place a high value on the family unit or the clan are often insulted by the individualistic Western pattern. They will label their young people who convert to Christ as rebellious or opportunist, because they have rejected the ancestors or the family. They have stepped out from under the elder's authority and therefore, from his blessing. Westerners often fail to realize that an individual decision in a group-oriented structure removes the convert from the social web that protects him. Many a Muslim has said, "I know that Isa is the Truth, but if I follow Him tonight, I won't have any food to eat tomorrow." Many married women are not permitted by their culture to make an individual and isolated decision about faith.

In describing this problem of cultural assumptions, Eugeniy Nedzelskiy explains the progress (or the lack of it) in evangelical protestant church growth in Russia and Eastern Europe.[8] He points out how the people subconsciously consider the leaders of the Eastern Church as the spiritual shareholders of the society. Although people may cordially accept the Message of the newcomers from the American protestant tradition, they will subconsciously be reluctant to respond from the depths of their heart until their elders, the Patriarchs of the Orthodox Church, demonstrate a positive attitude toward the Message. But this positive acceptance, according to Nedzelskiy, is not forthcoming so long as the evangelists ignore or avoid the culturally recognized spiritual decision makers.

6. Be sensitive to cultural decision-making signals

Be culturally appropriate. The Jerusalem Council of Acts 15 was held in order to determine whether Gentile converts to Christ should be required to submit to the Mosaic Law or not (Acts 15). The Judaizers measured true spirituality by circumcision and certain rules of abstinence. After hearing the arguments of missionaries to the Gentile converts and listening to the advice of the leader of the local congregation, the apostles wrote a letter to the Gentiles saying, "For it seemed good to the Holy Spirit and to us to lay upon you no greater burden than these essentials" (Acts 15:27). They had recognized that meeting certain physical requirements did not constitute true salvation and spirituality because these requirements would only hinder people from a deeper walk with Jesus in their cultural setting. This decision, in part, made possible the eventual transformation of a primarily Jewish Christian movement into a Gentile Christian movement. The apostles wisely distinguished between cultural hindrances that can be removed, and the Truth of the gospel that cannot be annulled.

We must demonstrate a lifestyle and approach that encourages people to follow Christ. Evaluate your life, conduct, and belief in order to weed out those habits and expectations that hinder true decision making. There are at least eight culture-bound signals that, if ignored, may affect decision making. Each one affects a cultural setting differently and these may, in some instances, not be relevant. Many more items could be mentioned, but the following are worthy of meditation, as they can hinder decisions for Christ.

A. The language of the messenger: Speak the language of their heart. If the language you use to explain the Truth is foreign to them, if it is not their heart language, they may reject the Message.

B. The method of evangelism: The way in which you present the Story often interprets the Message. If too much technology is used in the presentation people may make decisions in order to buy into that power. If the method overpowers the Message, such as use of certain Christian rock music in some Eastern European cultures, people will not listen. A medical outreach in some developing countries might lead people to believe because they will be assured of medical care. Aid to refugees coupled with a weak gospel presentation can cause people to come to Christ for the food. Verify that the Message being told by your methods is the Story you want them to hear.

C. The lifestyle and dress of the evangelist: Your appearance interprets or tells the Story. Some will become Christians in order to align themselves with the "cult of the cargo" that they see. Some may like the status that comes with Christ because of appearance.

Others will reject the Message because the clothing style of the messenger is not appropriate.

D. The style of worship: Every culture has subconscious and cultural definitions for worshiping the Supreme Being. The worship style you use says something about the value and credibility of the Message. For example, use musical instruments wisely. If a musical instrument is not culturally appealing, or if it is unknown, people will be distracted from the Message. They may have their own instruments, which will be more effective in leading them into worship.

E. The meeting place: Understand the cultural assumptions about the place where the host people meet God. A Christian-looking building will attract attention and persecution in some cultures. In other cultures, a structure that is tacky will detract. A non-church appearance, such as a storefront or warehouse, hinders some societies, whereas the absence of a meeting place will stop others.

F. The appeal to the wrong class: Choose the people you want to reach, and tailor your approach to their expectations. If your approach does not match the social expectation of the class, you may be ignored or shunned. Furthermore, in many societies the social group you attract directly affects the assembly's growth.

G. The code of behavior: You teach a code of Christian behavior by your conduct, dress, and language. You want the people to observe biblical behavior, but you might be revealing the cultural priorities of your own country. This could cause the followers to see Christianity as a foreign religion, especially if your codes do not make sense to them. H. L. Richard touches this in his study on India's cultures:

> Each convert extracted from his own cultural situation reinforces in the minds of the Hindus and Muslims the misunderstanding that Christians are opposed to their cultural traditions. In this sense, one could defend the thesis that each convert won from these faiths at present actually represents a setback to winning large numbers from these communities....

> There are areas where there can be no compromise with Hindu and Muslim cultures, but probably these areas are fewer than we

first think. Idolatry is an obvious area of conflict.... The same applies to caste....[9]

Biblical faith requires biblical holiness. This will hinder decisions for every people, but it should be a biblical hindrance rather than a cultural or foreign barrier.

H. The motives of the one responding: Encourage people to follow Christ for the best reason. Jesus admonished some because they wanted to follow Him for the wrong reasons (Matt. 8:18–22). Many wanted Jesus to prove His credibility with a miracle (Matt. 12:38; John 6:2, 14, 26, 30). Discern reasons why people want to follow Jesus, and be careful not to create the incorrect motivation. David Hesselgrave presents three types of motivation that may push people to make a decision.[10] First, there is the self-oriented motivation whereby the person is seeking Christ for a personal need or advantage. For example, some wanted Jesus to touch them for personal healing (Mark 1:40; 10:51). Second, there is the God-oriented motivation whereby the person makes a decision because of his new understanding of God. There may have been significant pre-evangelistic teaching that brought the people to see their spiritual condition, which pointed them to a desire to know God through Christ. A prime example of this is the God-fearing Cornelius (Acts 10). Third, there is the society-oriented motivation, whereby the person seeks the good of his community through the decision to follow Christ, as in the example of Zacchaeus (Luke 19:8–10). Following his encounter with Christ, the tax collector realized that he had been cheating his own people and returned what he had taken from them. His commitment to Jesus changed his relationship to his society.

7. Affirm the decision with follow-up teaching

Facilitate the way for followers to grow deeper into the knowledge of their new faith. The three thousand who chose to follow the Messiah in Acts 2 were baptized and integrated into the church. The early church's follow-up program was effective and the Holy Spirit "added to their number day by day those who were being saved" (Acts 2:47). It is clear that when people chose to follow the Messiah, they understood that they must learn more. And so the church of Berea was "more noble-minded than those in Thessalonica, for they received the word with great eagerness, examining the Scriptures daily" (Acts 17:11).

The person must continue to seek the good news even after he has found it. The Holy Spirit will give to him a deep desire to know the Truth—all of the Truth. You must use those approaches that are most effective in each setting to bring the new follower into deeper communion with Christ and the community of Christ. In some contexts, you may have to set up individual mentoring, depending on the social setting and personal needs of those who trust Christ. In other places, you will have to develop a community in which they will be accepted and nurtured. It may mean choosing a fellowship using the same language for worship. It may require that you plant a church with an ethnic quality all its own. New converts are seldom comfortable in a group where they do not recognize people. Unfamiliar faces can seem menacing and judgmental. If a family head has made a decision to follow Christ, he can be trained to lead prayers in his home with people he knows. As they mature in faith, they will be slowly introduced to others of similar language, culture, or conviction.

As you present the gospel, it is imperative that you respect the God-given ability to choose. Make every effort to remove cultural barriers that hinder understanding, at the same time speaking the Truth in love so that people come face to face with the One who will bring them peace and forgiveness. Then allow the Holy Spirit to convince them and bring them to the point of making a decision.

This Story Must Be Serious![11]

Jacques was sent by his district evangelism committee to plant a church among a people who practiced folk Islam. The people's skepticism of Jacques' motives made adjustment difficult, but once he and his family were acclimated to the new setting, they began building relationships. The district team, wanting to get the work moving faster, sent in their evangelism team to help Jacques. They showed the *Jesus* film in a mass meeting, but Jacques would not permit them to give a public invitation because he felt it was not time. He only let the team invite people to come and talk to him at their leisure.

Several days later the elders of the town came to see Jacques. They told him that at the end of the meeting, they were ready to "raise our finger to show our interest," but he had not asked them to do that.

"Why did you not do what others have done?" they asked.

Jacques told them that he wanted them to understand the Message before making a decision because this was an important decision. The old men walked away shaking their heads and saying to one another, "We had better listen more carefully next time. This must be serious!"

Several months later the same elders gave full support to the Message, and a church was planted in their community.

As the adage says, you can take a horse to the water but you can't make it drink. So too, the decision for Christ must be a personal one. Every refusal or acceptance leading to a change of behavior is not simply the result of a clearly presented Message. It happens because the person has seen justifiable cause to change his mind. As people entrusted with the Message, we must be faithful in presenting the Story in a way that will enable the listener to make a decision in culturally appropriate manner. The decision that follows will transform him!

Chapter 6

The Crisis of an Indigenous Church

Establish a church that focuses on Christ

OUR CHURCH IS finally self-supporting!" exclaims the treasurer to the church council after one year of paying the bills. "Self-supporting" is the benchmark of a mature church, a goal that the leaders of this church are pursuing.

"We make our own decisions," says the lead elder to the district administrator. He knows that one measure of an adult congregation is "self-governing," and he wants the administrator to know that his church is capable of making their own decisions.

"Look at all the new people! That's proof that we are viable church." This leader has to assure his people that they are doing something well. After all, who can argue with increasing numbers when a church is "self-propagating?"

The crisis develops when the sent-one wants the newly established church to take full responsibility for its life and well-being. In some cases, the local leaders believe that they will never match up to the criteria of a mature church, especially if theirs must function like the missionary's home church. Others may not feel free to make their own decisions because they must cater to the pressure of foreign income. In essence, the local believers do not see themselves as a viable church without the presence of the foreign worker. What can be done from the outset to avoid this stagnation in maturity?

The "Three-Self" Measure of a Church

The "three-self" concept, now including the fourth one, "self-theologizing," has been the standard for measuring church maturity for more than a hundred years. It has served well. Whether in cross-cultural work or in mono-cultural church multiplication, this tool has helped local churches and administrative leadership to determine the progress of a congregation toward spiritual maturity. The three-self principle has been so effective that even the Maoist government used it to officially approve the Christian church in China.

Although these terms are helpful, it is time to ask if the three-self measure of the indigenous church is true to Scripture. The goal of the next three chapters is to propose a description of the indigenous church that uses Christ as the measure of a mature church. Christ-centered focus assumes that the Church[1] is composed of people of every culture who trust Christ as Savior and Lord. This multi-ethnic picture is what the Apostle John saw standing in front of the throne, singing praises to the Lamb of God (Rev. 7:9). These people are the Church, even if their local congregations may not have gathered in expensive buildings. Their maturity was not measured by power or position, but by a love for Christ demonstrated in everyday life.

Henry Venn, the missionary statesman of the nineteenth century, presented a new way to measure a church's success. He proposed that local congregations or church unions that support their own ministry should be "self-supporting." When congregations have mature leaders who lead them in spiritual and administrative life, they are "self-governing." In addition, when assemblies continue to make disciples through evangelism, they are "self-propagating." Venn's premise was that mission societies would be able to determine the time to turn the work over to local people by using these three measurements.

A closer look at Venn's concept reveals that the way to measure an assembly's maturity is to compare it to "self." The use of the term "self" before each definition suggests that "I support," "I govern," or "I propagate." Although there is truth in this, and even though this is set in contrast to being ruled by the sent-one or the mission agency, the self-focused title causes one to look at himself or at others. By nature, humans compare themselves to something or someone. This is sometimes carried to the extreme, so that people can be handicapped by worrying about what others think about them. As a consequence, the very prefix "self" begs comparison by asking, "Whom am *I* supposed to look like?"

The church planter or the sent-one comes into the new or cross-cultural situation and gathers new believers around him. He comes with the image of his sending church and sending culture in his mind, and his home church often becomes a subconscious picture of what the newly planted church should look like. It is normal that new believers subsequently look to the church planter to define their maturity. This becomes more critical when the new converts ask how they can become a "church." They will tend to compare their assembly with the foreign worker's church, as if it is the model of maturity to emulate. As a result, the sending church's character is often what defines the self-governing, self-supporting, self-propagating church.

Take, for example, the self-governing aspect. The leader of the new congregation in Africa wants to know how a local church council is selected in the missionary's home church. In response, the sent-one from North America describes how the Nominating Committee receives candidates, and then how the assembly elects new members. Africans often are amazed at this democratic process because "general elections" do not always work this way in African chieftain cultures. In an Asian country, there may be a different discovery. The sent-one describes how a leader works with his committee to enact decisions that are accepted by a "majority" vote, even if there may be a dissenting voice or two. The listeners are confused because they decide according to a consensual decision-making process that ultimately becomes the decision of the leader, sometimes without a vote ever being cast. Their different culturally informed process causes the leaders to ask if they are truly a mature church because they do not govern like the "mother church." Their eyes are focused on another cultural model.

The church that wants to be self-propagating asks the foreign mentor how to "do evangelism." They want to learn how to expand like his church grows. Being from another culture with highly developed technology, the sent-one tells them about radio evangelism or complex multi-church campaigns run by joint committees and much publicity. He also may share with them how a "viable church" sends missionaries to foreign lands. From this description, the local believers assess their resources: they do not have electricity for open-air campaigns, much less a transmitter for radio evangelism, and they cannot afford the salary and travel fare to send a foreign missionary. While they do tell their friends about Christ in a person-to-person and heart-to-heart manner, they have to admit that they are not self-propagating like the mother church. Hence they conclude that they are not truly mature.

The self-support criterion is most obvious in the less affluent cultures. The Westerner goes to the developing country full of enthusiasm about reaching the culture in the most efficient manner. He decides that training local leaders is the quickest way to effect growth and maturity so he provides money to send a prime candidate to seminary or other specialized education. When the graduate returns home, he suddenly does not fit. He discovers that he has learned many new things that "cannot be done here." And the home congregation grimly states, "He does not have our heart anymore." As a consequence, they conclude that they are not self-supporting because they cannot afford the graduate's living standard. They think that they can only be self-supporting with the help of the mother church.

The assumption often carried to other cultures is that the sending culture does church correctly. When this presupposition drives the church planter to coach a new assembly to maturity, it can lead the new believers to evaluate themselves in the image of the home church rather than in the image of Christ. In some cases, they may become confused, thinking that Christ-likeness means being like the sending culture. They begin to see themselves as an extension of the foreign mission agency. In some cases, when the expatriate missionary must evacuate due to war or another crisis, the believers may think that they are not a viable church because the missionaries are no longer present.

Would it not have been better to teach the believers to be Christ-dependent in all things? Tom Julien clarifies one source of this misplaced identity in his essay on "The Essence of the Church." Julien states:

> The fundamental problem in church planting is our tendency to identify the church with her cultural expression rather than her biblical essence, making that cultural expression the norm.[2]

I contend that this cultural expression becomes the focal point because we started with the wrong image of the end product.

The German missiologist, Peter Beyerhaus, writes about this danger inherent in the traditional definition of the self-defined indigenous church. He correctly states that our understanding of self has been spoiled by the Fall (Gen. 3). It is for this reason that we are invited to be "crucified with Christ" by placing Him at the center of our being (Gal. 2:20). An individual who asserts self in a church causes great danger to that congregation. It is possible for a church to function without Christ at the center, especially if the believers define the assembly on the basis of self. Dr. Beyerhaus proposes that the church must be developed in "a grateful awareness that all the resources of the Church are in Christ, her Head ..."[3]

The Apostle Paul writes that the Church owes its existence and being to Christ. In Ephesians 1, Paul identifies some important "focus sets" concerning Christ and His Church. We are blessed in Christ (v. 3) because He chose us in Him before the foundation of the world (v. 4). His plan is that we be holy and blameless in His sight (v. 4), which is His act of love. Our holiness is enhanced because Christ changed our status as orphans to that of His adopted sons and daughters, made possible through the sacrifice of His blood (v. 7). And as if that were not enough, God has shown us the mystery of His will in Christ (v. 8). To insure that this promise is kept in our lives, He has sealed the pledge of His inheritance by the Holy Spirit (1:13–14). Is it any wonder that we are told in Colossians, "Christ is before all things, and in Him all things hold together" (1:17)?

The principles of Scripture are culturally transferable and filled with grace because they tie spiritual goals to God's Word. If Christ is the head of the Body (Eph. 1:21–23), and He sustains His Church (Col. 1:15–20), then we should teach the emerging congregation that they are mature in Christ because of their full trust in Him. They should believe that they are able to do all things through Christ (Phil. 4:19), even reach spiritual maturity as the church in a different location. They should focus on being so possessed by Christ that they pursue adulthood in Him and measure their growth by His Word.

The Church exists because of Christ and for Christ. Without Christ, there is no Church. The converse is also true: with Christ, there is the Church. We err when speaking in terms of "going to church" or "inviting people to church." The Church is not a building but a composition of those who are in Christ. Our identity is in

Christ, not in a human-made organization. Those who are in Christ are an expression of Christ. As a consequence, on the human level, we cannot measure the worth or maturity of a congregation by referring to self. We need to refer to Christ and His standard of measurement.

The congregation whose focus is on Christ will more profoundly grasp their faith and ministry as a personal commitment. They will look to Christ, who makes them a part of the universal Church, without the limitations of cultural circumstances, extra-biblical traditions, or individual personalities. The believers know that their identity is tied to the One who daily transforms their lives. These believers will see their conviction as a personal commitment to Christ, without foreign cultural baggage, because He is the Way and the Truth. Over the long term, the growth of this church will be spontaneous because the adherents recognize their maturity in Christ rather than in self.

The church planter must refocus his assumptions about the church being established. As a sent-one to another culture, he must believe that the new assembly is the Church. He adheres to an ecclesiology that believes that the national church is capable of demonstrating Christ-centered qualities from the time of birth. Both the sending church and the local congregation are a "national church"[4] within the universal Body of Christ. Although the sent-one represents his sending church, he must see the newly planted church as an equal expression of Christ. And when the missionary no longer resides in the host country, the remaining believers will see themselves as a local body that relates to the sending church as a local and national church. This understanding of the church can also prevent missionaries and new believers from behaving like a mission child who only relates to the sending body in a filial manner.

A Christ-centered focus for the believers will also enhance spontaneous growth because people will be measuring themselves by Christ's expectation for growth rather than the expectations of a foreign assembly in another country. True church growth cannot be programmed by methods, although some men and women are capable of growing a church. Rather, church growth is something that the Holy Spirit does in His time and way through frail human instruments. As Jesus told Nicodemus, "The wind blows where it wishes and you hear the sound of it, but you do not know where it comes from and where it is going; so is every one who is born of the Spirit" (John 3:8). Although we cannot tell the Holy Spirit to make us a spontaneous movement, and even though Jesus promises to build *His* Church (Matt. 16:18), we are warned to not "quench the Spirit" (1 Thess. 5:10). Our desire is to be those who encourage the moving of the Holy Spirit through our church-planting ministry. When our mental image of a mature church is focused on Christ's person, we open the door to seek His affirmation rather than that of the sending culture or the church planter.

We need to renew our vision of what the New Testament church looked like. We will clarify our assumptions about today's church by studying the early church, seeing those people's convictions in their cultural context. We must learn the values to which the first Christians adhered, which made their life in Christ become a spontaneous movement. From this model, we can formulate the qualities that define a mature Christ-focused church.

The Primitive Church Models Spontaneous Growth

The first century church was truly dynamic in growth and it had a powerful impact on its society. Its focus was to know Christ and to make Him known and it was within this ambiance that the Spirit was free to build His Church. The core values of the early church functioned together to make them the Christ-centered church. Within this setting, the believers measured themselves to Christ's expectations. In this section we will examine their core characteristics, with a view to seeing how Christ is our measure of wholeness.

The book of Acts encourages us with the account of the boldness and tenacity of the early believers. Honest and accurate, Luke's story highlights of the spontaneous growth of the church during its first thirty years. The "Christ-ones" faced seemingly impossible odds, yet the first century world listened to them. The followers were persecuted, but in spite of tremendous opposition, new people continued to join their ranks.

The apostles and disciples proclaimed their faith, which enabled the Christian movement to survive and expand. This valuable Truth-experience could not be removed, destroyed, or sold. It could only be given away to another person who would, in turn, grasp it for himself or herself. These early believers practiced five behavioral convictions that were the source of their spontaneous growth, and assured that each one owned the faith.

1. Followers of Jesus repented and were baptized

Each believer had to undergo these two points of commitment in order to complete the transformation process called conversion. Repentance required one to renounce old belief and conduct. Each individual had to willingly leave old ways behind. If necessary, believers had to correct past wrongs that affected family members or friends. This entailed confessing one's personal responsibility for the sins that had dominated their life in the past.

Baptism openly declared to friends that the past was being buried, that the new believer was now cleansed by Jesus' sacrifice, and that he or she would be walking in a new lifestyle. Baptism was a confession that the former way of life was wrong and that the new Truth about Jesus had become creed for life's conduct.

One did not become a follower of Jesus by birth, by conscription, by ordinance, or by any other means except a personal conversion, which included personal repentance and submission to baptism. The citizens of Samaria had to repent and be baptized, which they did in large numbers (Acts 8:12). The government official from Ethiopia had to repent and be baptized, which he eagerly sought (Acts 8:38). Saul repented and was baptized (Acts 9:18). Cornelius and his household repented and were baptized (Acts 10:48).

When people confess that their misery and sin are their fault, when they humble themselves before God who is greater than them and admit that they need His help, something begins to happen in their heart and mind. The act of correcting past wrongs causes one to realize that their behavior is a personal responsibility for which they are accountable to a Savior, and not a human group. Almost everyone who passes through these steps will own their convictions and be more careful in future choices.

2. Followers of Jesus obeyed the Holy Spirit in every life experience

The apostles had lived and observed Jesus for three years. At His ascension, He reminded them that they would be witnesses of these things. He promised them that His physical presence would be replaced by the Holy Spirit, who would come upon all of them in power. The disciples waited for the Holy Spirit in a private room, and when the He came upon them, they were transformed.

Peter, formerly impatient and brusque, became the leader who spoke when prompted by the Holy Spirit. At Pentecost, he spoke to a large crowd (Acts 2). In the temple, he boldly talked of Christ, causing the astonished leaders to ask where he had been educated (Acts 4). He confronted the deception of Ananias and Sapphira with the help of penetrating Spirit discernment (Acts 5:3).

Philip, the lay evangelist, moved from Samaria to Gaza because the Spirit sent him (Acts 8:29). Ananias of Damascus went to minister to the newly converted Saul because the Spirit sent him (Acts 9:10). Throughout the story of the new church, people intentionally responded to the guidance of the Holy Spirit. This obedience gave the believers liberty to do what they knew in their hearts was God's will. It freed them from the fear of the unknown, giving them courage to step out in faith to do great deeds for Jesus. Their boldness issued out of the knowledge that they belonged to Jesus, and that He, through the Holy Spirit, lived within them. The One who by faith transformed them now lived in them.

3. Followers of Jesus integrated themselves into the worship and teaching of the apostles

We note that the three thousand who were converted on the day of Pentecost "were continually devoting themselves to the apostles' teaching and to fellowship, to the breaking of bread and to prayer" (Acts 2:42). And "*every day*, in the temple and from house to house, they kept right on teaching and preaching Jesus as the Christ" (Acts 5:42, emphasis added).

Worship and teaching were not options; they were required as a part of the conversion commitment. It was out of this community experience that the individual believer matured and was later sent out to engage others. This sense of unity helped assure the new believer that he belonged to a movement that was larger than himself. It gave him a structure of accountability in which he could develop and mature. This *koinonia* increased the bond of ownership of the faith.

One of the key teaching events of the first century church worship was the Lord's Table. The believers were baptized and immediately became active in corporate worship, which included "the breaking of bread and prayer... And day by day continuing with one mind in the temple, and breaking bread from house to house..." (Acts 2:42, 46). Their fellowship with one another was an experience of teaching and joyful praise. They not only shared their meals, but they also focused worship on the Lord of the *agapé* meal, or the "Lord's Supper" (1 Cor. 11:20). These meals were patterned after the instruction of Jesus given on the Passover night. Their celebration aimed at remembering Jesus through the elements or symbols of the bread and wine of the cup (Matt. 26:28–30; Luke 22:14–20; 1 Cor. 11:20–34).

This event was an act of worship for all believers. In the early church, all believers were baptized; therefore, it was not limited to church members but given to all followers. The event was an identifying feature for all who were in the faith. It was a daily (or at least regular) affirmation of each individual's belonging to Jesus, partaking in His suffering, rejoicing in His resurrection, and looking forward to His coming.

4. Followers of Jesus gave personal testimony to the resurrected Christ

Jesus commissioned His followers to tell others the story of their experience. Each believer told his circle of friends about the change that took place upon committing to the Messiah. The conversion process enabled the believer to openly demonstrate that transforming conviction. Transformed behavior gave credence to what each one said. The witness and evangelism of the early church was not a duty of one class of believers. It belonged to each one and to everyone.

To the political and religious opposition of their day, they confessed, "We cannot stop speaking what we have seen and heard" (Acts 4:20). They were so gripped by this Truth that, when flogged or persecuted, they "went on their way rejoicing that they had been considered worthy to suffer shame for His name" (Acts 5:41). As we continue reading Luke's story, we note how many times the common "lay person" (to use a contemporary expression) and the apostles "scattered" and "preached" and people "believed and were baptized."[5]

5. Followers of Jesus shared the ministry of leading a group

As the Christian group increased in size, they had to organize themselves. They appointed deacons to handle the distribution of food so that the apostles could dedicate themselves to prayer and Bible teaching (Acts 6:1–7). Later they sent out their best leaders, Paul and Barnabas, to plant churches in other unreached areas (Acts 13:1–6). James and Peter (Acts 15:7, 13) and others were also recognized as leaders. Paul organized local leadership in the Christian communities he developed across Asia Minor and Europe.

Leadership was not limited to a hierarchical, exclusive group of a few individuals. Instead, each one was enabled to lead in his or her area of giftedness. Each Christian had a role to perform in their group. Some did become leaders of a larger group. They were called apostles, evangelists, pastors, teachers, elders, deacons, and deaconesses. The duty was shared in the true sense of the priesthood of all believers.

The believers who met, prayed, and worked together held the church as if it belonged to them. Their numbers increased exponentially at such a pace that the Luke was unable to give precise numbers. We remark Luke's statement that there were three thousand at Pentecost (Acts 2:41), then five thousand (Acts 4:4), after which multitudes of men and women were added (Acts 5:14). Finally, the disciples increased greatly (Acts 6:7), Samaria believed (Acts 8:12), and the whole region learned and responded (Acts 13:49).

We know of the impact of the early church because church history informs us that transformed people went home to established viable communities of faith in Libya, Egypt, Ethiopia, and into Arabia. At the opening of the second century, the Christian group had reached as far west as France and Spain, as far to the east as India, and north to Macedonia. They did all of this without cars, radios, TVs, or the Internet!

Qualities of the Christ-Focused Church

Anyone who doubts the integrity of this Message would not be inclined to do what these people did. People will not endure two centuries of persecution in order to protect a lie. There was something in this gospel that was worth dying for. These believers would not have spent money to convene councils designed to safeguard the gospel Truth from errors if that truth was not worth keeping. These people owned the Truth of Christ. They saw themselves as belonging to Christ and Christ to them. Their faith belonged to them and no one could take it away. Their belief was so real that it fit in the culture through their habits. Although following Christ caused conflict and cultural stress, it always transformed people and cultures for the better. These believers could only conform their belief and lifestyle, and ultimately the culture, to the image of Christ. The church was indigenous because Christ was in the Church. From the example of the early church we find those qualities that insured its viability. The Catholic missiologist, Pedro Aruppe, calls it the "inculturated Church":

> Inculturation is the incarnation of Christian life and message in a concrete cultural area in such a way that this experience not only comes to express itself with the elements proper to the culture in question (which would only be a superficial adaptation) but becomes an inspiring, normative, and unifying principle that transforms and re-creates the culture, giving rise to a "new creation."[6]

In his book, *Signs of the Spirit*, Howard Snyder describes the common habits of renewal movements that were critical to building synergy within God's people. He begins with the first century church as the base that leads him to conclusions he draws from the Pietist, Moravian, and Methodist movements. These all progressed as spontaneous events because they emphasized a personal relationship with Christ that leads to holy living, small group encounters for worship and Bible study, and trained lay leaders who affirmed and extended the work.[7]

We want our contemporary churches to demonstrate the same life-giving habits. The qualities for the adult church that are true to Scripture are intended to help us focus on the kind of church that

Christ wants us to plant, rather than holding up ourselves or our sending culture as the image to imitate. With this in mind, I propose four criteria for measuring the Christ-centered church. These four keep the pattern of the historic Venn-Anderson definition of an indigenous church, which was more sociologically framed. The four criteria are born from the New Testament example, while taking into account the sociological nature of the Church. They help our people focus on what Christ desires from them. As these qualities are taught and applied to the local congregation, they become the source of encouragement because the gathering of Christ's followers is seeking to be like Him. These four criteria or qualities are:

1) The worship-giving church

2) The witness-mission church

3) The teaching-training church

4) The leading-serving church

Each of these qualities interconnects with the others. None applies a culturally bound measurement to determine church maturity. Each quality builds the mindset that enhances spontaneous growth. Chapters 7 and 8 will describe these four qualities in detail. Appendix B presents an evaluation tool that will help believers assess their focus on Christ, the Head of their church.

Rodriguez Finds What He Cannot Keep[8]

Stories about the sudden growth of the Church are being told and heard all over the world. They have similar characteristics that tell us why they are expanding. I conclude with one example from South America that shows the importance of people maintaining the right focus. This testimony, therefore, is a composite of many people's experience.

Rodriguez was born into a "cultural-Christian" family. The local padre baptized his ten brothers and sisters. They attended Mass on the special days and participated in the holidays to the Virgin Mary. He considered himself Christian because his parents were Christian.

It was at work that he first heard that Jesus is more than the benevolent "son of Mary" who hung on a sacrificial cross. His coworker was consistently joyful, he was believable, he spoke truthfully, and he loved talking about Jesus, the Son of God. In time, Rodriguez went to visit his friend's place of worship to see what this religion was all about. People met in a small warehouse. They sang with exuberance and prayed as if they knew God personally. They hugged one another as if they were family. People in the warehouse were even healed of illness right there during the meeting. A man (and sometimes a woman) taught them from the stories of the Bible, a book that Rodriguez was not permitted to read. Rodriguez found himself being drawn to something he did not have.

One day it hit him like a bolt of lightning: "Jesus died and rose from the dead so that I, Rodriguez, can have forgiveness of sins and new life!" He knelt with his friend and spoke a prayer placing his trust in Jesus as his Savior. That was the beginning of his new life.

Rodriguez was immediately integrated into a community study group where people experienced in a microcosm what was happening in the larger warehouse meetings. When Rodriguez felt a burden to reach his own family, the lay pastor encouraged him to share his newfound faith with them. He did this and was thrilled that they, too, wanted Jesus. His lay pastor encouraged him to begin praying and reading the Bible with his extended family in his home, which he did.

But then, a problem arose: the neighbors also wanted to attend! The lay leader encouraged Rodriguez to get some Bible training at a night Bible school so that he could be better equipped to lead his home Bible group. This training helped him gain confidence in his ministry and increased his knowledge of Christ. As a consequence, the home worship group continued to increase in size until it was divided, forming a second group. Rodriguez' experience was also taking place in many other communities all over the city. Growth was spontaneous because the faith was in Christ, as biblically expressed in their culture.

This experience is a worldwide phenomenon being repeated in groups of people whose focus is on Christ. You, too, can lead believers to partner with the Spirit as they look to Christ for their church's identity.

The next two chapters describe the four criteria of the mature church in terms their focus on Christ. These descriptions grow out of the principles demonstrated by the early church. Applying the four qualities will enable followers of Jesus in the church today to see themselves as an expression of Christ's Body as they find liberty to mature in the faith that they can call their own.

Chapter 7

The Crisis of Worship and Witness

Experience the immanent Christ in worship and witness

THE CONGREGATION THAT experiences an immanent Christ through their expression of worship will naturally demonstrate compassion for those outside of their group. Such an assembly will have a profound impact upon the culture. When you are establishing a congregation, how do you enable them to worship and witness in a culturally appropriate way? How do you encourage them to sing, pray, preach, and teach in ways that make sense to them, rather than appeal to you, the outsider? Missionaries often experience tension when they encounter unfamiliar worship forms, which may be acceptable to the local culture but which were not found back home. This chapter will describe guidelines that enable a group of people to pursue worship and witness that is Christ-focused. But first, let us look at what is happening in one part of the world where worship is Christ-focused.

Miracle in Hunon Province[1]

Mr. Yu grew up on a collective farm in Hunon Province of China. The Communist Party ensured that everyone worked for the improvement of the state and the commune. Yu had never heard of Christians until some strangers joined his work group. They had been transferred from another region and quickly integrated into the community. Yu noticed that the newcomers were different. They were content, they expressed joy, they did not seem to worry about the unknown, and they often sang as they worked in the fields. Their songs spoke about a certain man who came to earth, who suffered and died for all humanity, and who did not stay in the grave. What surprised Yu most was how the songs encouraged people to persevere by simply trusting this man they called Jesus.

One day Yu asked the men about the songs, and he was invited to the home of one of the singers to hear more. It was in this home that Yu heard the whole story of Jesus, the Deliverer. He placed his trust in Jesus, and discovered the same joy and ability to persevere that he had seen in the members of his commune. Slowly, a miracle began to occur in his life. His anger toward the Communist Party diminished. He found inner peace. Even when he was transferred to a much larger city, he was not fearful. He knew that the Truth he had learned about Jesus in the home group would keep him safe. Furthermore, the worship leader promised him that the Lord would guide him to a group of Christians in the big city.

By the time Yu was settled in his new city, he became aware that many social changes were taking place. The grip of the authority figures was not as strong as expected—at least not in his part of town. The economy was picking up, and his job was better than before. One day, as he walked by a tall apartment building, he heard singing. It reminded him of the songs he had learned in the worship group in Hunon. He followed the sound until he had reached a room near the main street. The doors were open and the room was filled with people singing and encouraging one another. The room was charged with joy, and Yu knew that he had found a home for his soul. These were his people, even though he did not know anyone.

Worship-Giving

Jesus taught that those who worship must do so "in spirit and in truth" (John 4:4). The focus of one's worship will determine the focus of his or her life-walk. Worship is a close-to-the-heart spiritual event that is deeply influenced by cultural expectations. Singing and praise, prayer and prophecy, Scripture reading and preaching, reading the apostolic letters, making collections for the poor, and celebrating the Lord's Supper, all characterized the worship of the early church. The attitudes of worship were humility, reverence, gratefulness, joyfulness, and orderliness. The believers were exhorted to continually offer up a "sacrifice of praise" to God (Heb. 13:15).

A worship-giving church is a community of believers who focus their prayer and praise on Christ. Through their worship (Col. 3:13–

17), they mature in their expression of spiritual gifts (Eph. 4:11–16), always aiming for the smooth and unified growth of the body. They seek always to bring glory and honor to the name of Christ through their songs, praise, prayer, teaching, and giving (Eph. 5:18–20). This requires that worship contribute to the growth of the believers and to the unity of the Body (Eph. 4:1–3). It does not require specific forms, languages, or styles. Rather, it permits those elements of worship to be determined by the believers' understanding of Scripture, their knowledge of God, and by their way of responding to Him, so that all is done for the glory of God and the honor of the Lord Jesus (Col. 3:17).

The worshiping church is a congregation of believers whose response is a living sacrifice of all that they possess, including their time, energies, ministry, and service (Rom. 12:1–2). They give out of their possessions (2 Cor. 8:2), and they give joyfully, abundantly, and lovingly (2 Cor. 8:2, 8, 14), in ways appropriate to their culture. They distribute or invest their wealth according to the biblical ethic as it applies in their socio-economic context.

The New Testament gives us a small picture of what took place in the worship gathering. Although little is said about the appearance of the place of worship, we know that the people met in homes. We note that the attitude of the heart is far more important than the posture or method of worship. When we plant churches cross-culturally, we should help believers understand certain attitudes are necessary to worshiping God. There are certain acts of worship that believers must incorporate into a relationship with God. A wise leader will help members of the assembly find those culturally mean-ingful worship forms that bring honor to God. Incorrect habits or attitudes, often motivated by cultural expectations, can be culled out with wisdom and a spirit of humility.

This measure of the worship-giving church does not preclude or presuppose a certain budget. It does not suggest financial power, strategy, or programs. Rather, the local emerging assembly deter-mines its own financial capability and expression by obedience to the Bible. The believers' manner of sharing and giving is expressed in a way that makes sense in the context of their culture while remaining within the expectations of Scripture. This principle expects that the foreign worker will not establish costly worship programs that the local church may not deem important, programs that the local people are not able to support on their own and that will hinder spontaneous growth.

A minimum of six factors contextualizes Christ-focused worship and enhances spontaneous growth. Let us briefly consider each one.

1. The environment for meeting together must lend itself to worship

The place of worship or physical location needs to lead to Christ in a way that permits people the freedom and security to encounter God. If cultural religious experience insists that there be a chapel or meeting hall, then a worship place should be built. Some countries will not permit the construction or use of an official meeting place. In other countries, political persecution is so intense that a building raises undue suspicion. In such cases, people need to learn to worship in homes or low-profile assembly halls.

The place of worship should be a safe haven, enabling worshipers to sense the immanent presence of God with His people. Upon entering this place, a visitor should be able to tell that God's people meet here. The appearance of the building, if it is visible, will send a message to both believers and outsiders. Although this cultural expectation of appearance may inform the choices for construction, worldly values should not guide the architecture or decision-making. The knowledge of Christ and His Word must be the chief guide.

Seating style should be in keeping with cultural practices. Former Muslims may prefer sitting on floor mats, whereas Europeans and Latin Americans may prefer the benches or chairs, like in a cathedral. Former Hindu or Buddhist believers may choose more meditative styles. Whether women are placed on one side and men on the other, or if men and women are seated together, it should be the decision of the local people. The seating arrangement must be the preference of the people and not the sent-one.

The cultural understanding of time and space will also affect the choice of worship center and determine how people spend the time in God's presence. Meeting in a temple or church building needs to be the decision of the Christians who must build it and maintain it. It is imperative that the building be financed and cared for by the Christians who use it. They declare their faith through this building. It is their faith that becomes visible in persecution.

The church planter may give input into these things, although the owners of the faith—the people who meet here—must make all final decisions.

2. The language of worship must belong to the heart

The language of the heart of the majority ethnic group should be the language of worship. Translations into a secondary language should be avoided whenever possible. Songs, Scripture reading, prayer, and teaching should all be in the heart language of the hearers. This contributes to local ownership of the event and enhances people's desire to become part of what is happening.

A mutually spoken language can be used if several ethnic groups consistently attend, but even this language needs to be chosen carefully. If the trade language is used rather than the mother tongue, and if this trade language belonged to a former oppressor or invading people, the worship experience may be hampered. If and when several groups are present, leaders should provide moments when each ethnic group will meet alone for prayer and teaching, as well as gathering in a larger group. The people should not feel that they worship a foreign God who is unable to speak their heart language.

Some countries have a middle class population that uses the government language more freely than their mother tongue. The church planting team that is seeking to establish the church among this sector of the population should use the language that is most common to this social class. Bear in mind, however, that the language of worship will exclude other classes, just as the vernacular language would eliminate groups of people. In the final analysis, the local assembly needs to make the language decision that will best enhance worship as well as touch the lives of non-believers.

3. The music must belong to the culture

Music that speaks to the heart of the people will increase their desire to worship and will motivate them to share their faith with others, because it sounds like their faith. A team member with training or experience in ethnomusicology will greatly enhance the worship of the people if he or she can enable them to create their own hymnology that sounds like their kind of music and teaches God's Truth in their language images. Some missionaries of the past have taken Western hymnology to cultures that do not sing that style of music. Many of those ethnic groups have, over generations, adapted this music to their native rhythm and sound, and those who grew up in the Christian faith often find these songs very meaningful, even if the music sounds different to their cultural ears.

In his article on "Trends on Global Worship," Frank Fortunato states that church planting teams are recognizing the importance of having someone who is a musician and artist in their midst. An artist's contribution to the development of the new assembly will significantly enhance the spontaneous growth of the gospel among the new people group.[2] *Pioneers* is one ministry that seeks to include individuals on their teams who know how to mobilize and disciple local worship leaders.[3] It is well worth the time of the church planter to network with other groups or individuals who can help the emerging church develop a biblical hymnology that teaches Scripture and reaches out to others.

4. Teaching patterns and styles in worship must be sensitive to the culture

Every culture lives by its philosophy or conviction of teaching and learning. It may take the foreigner many years to fully learn how the host culture communicates didactic material. Study of cultural teaching methods, natural educational settings, public rhetoric style, and thought pattern, will enhance the sent-one's ability to communicate publicly. It is presumptuous to believe that all people listen and learn in the same way as we who are from the West. For example, not everyone thinks in a three-point Western homiletical sermon! On the other hand, not all cultures follow cyclical logic. Some cultures move easily from abstract to concrete thought, whereas others find it hard to grasp the abstractions. The thought pattern that is common to the culture is the approach that will most effectively communicate God's Truth. People will joyfully come to hear a speaker who communicates the gospel their way.

Leaders of the emerging church must be quickly encouraged and trained to lead and teach in worship using their own style of oral communication. The more they are involved in worship, the faster it will be owned and the more intimate it will become to each believer.

5. Giving must be a part of worship

The Scriptures teach that joyful giving and generous contributions are the norm for believers. Therefore, we must teach biblical principles for giving and money management. We need to help the congregations determine how their culture gives to royalty and, in turn, how they would give to Jesus, the King of kings. Let us help them understand that the awe that comes from worshiping God leads to self-sacrifice. We must develop a style of giving in worship that meets their need but is also the requirement of Scripture.

Giving should be seen as God's way of empowering the local assembly to accomplish greater outreach and caring for the Kingdom. Hence, the believers need to see tangible activity accruing from their generosity. This will have direct influence on the joy and liberality of giving. People give joyfully when they see the purpose for which they give, and we must encourage financial self-reliance and accountability between those who give and those who manage the finances.

Church planters must teach biblical principles and guidelines, always encouraging holiness, reverence, cleanliness, and orderliness in worship, as these might apply to giving. For example, if you are from a less expressive culture, you may have to suppress some of your own reaction against your host country's style of giving, especially if their offering requires dancing, singing, or demonstration. On the other hand, if your church of origin uses a small donation box in a hidden corner, you may discover that the adopted culture sees this approach as demeaning to their understanding of God.

6. The Lord's Supper is a focused worship event

The Lord's Supper celebrates the living Lord drawing all believers to focus on the One who daily forgives and leads them. As baptism confesses a break with the past life and frees the believer to follow Jesus, so the Table affirms the daily victory that one experiences when following Him.

This act of worship needs to be a local or family spiritual event. Believing heads of families or cell groups should be trained to lead their local assembly in periods of praise, testimony, prayer, affirmation, and remembrance of Jesus around the Table. All who confess Jesus as Savior should be able to participate. This group intimacy should confirm the priesthood of all believers rather than elevate the clergy. As the barometer of church life, this event should be the focal experience of intimacy with Christ and the Body that motivates believers to walk in holiness as Jesus did. Alex Hay quotes J. Bolton's study entitled "What is the Purpose of the Lord's Supper?"

> It would seem that neglect of the Lord's Supper, the failure practically to recognize its central place in the life and worship of the Church, the forms and ceremonies currently employed, and the situation which prohibits the people from functioning as priests by participating whole-heartedly in worship, are reasons for the powerlessness of the evangelical church today. The time may not be far distant when an increasing apostasy and a complete decline in spirituality may in many cases force true believers again to the simplicity of the "Church in the house" as in the days of the apostles. Without pomp or earthly glamour or form, Christians will again gather around the symbol of the Savior's death and so worship Him in simplicity and in truth. The leadership of these meetings will not be relegated to a presiding clergy, but the Holy Spirit will lead through the Christians present.[4]

Note that on the evaluation tool in Appendix B, the characteristics attributed to the worship-giving criteria do not describe programs or financially supported events. Rather, these criteria focus on biblical attitudes and actions that the Christ-centered church incorporates into its conviction. These are culturally transferable and enhance obedience to Christ.

Witness-Mission

Jesus did not ordain committees to plan evangelism but He sent individuals to share with other people what they had seen and heard. Believers in the early church were compelled to speak of what they had heard and seen (Acts 4:20). In his letter to persecuted churches, the Apostle John states that "what we have seen and heard we declare to you ... that your joy might be full" (1 John 1:3–4). This phrase expresses the behavior of the witness. He talks about what he has experienced in a way that it gives joy to his audience. It is good news (*evangel*).

A witness-mission church is a congregation whose believers claim the mandate of the gospel declaration as their first priority in the discipling process (Matt. 28:18–20). They see the masses with the same heart of compassion that Jesus did (Matt. 9:36), and recognize that each believer is empowered by the Holy Spirit to declare the message of the Kingdom (Acts 1:8). They make it their business to disciple all the nations, beginning with their area of primary influence. As their assembly grows in number, they continue to expand to new people and nations (Acts 13:1–12). The local church should develop its vision for mission, beginning with its earliest steps of development. Mission should be taught as an integral part of the church, beginning at the birth of the assembly. Cross-cultural evangelism should be developed and financially supported by the emerging church, not by the missionary or his sending organization. Sent-ones should be concerned less about how they organize themselves than that they are pursuing their own ways to reach the lost. This measure does not preclude or presuppose any technology, finance, committee, or method to help the assembly be missionary minded. It presents no foreign example of missionary to them with the expectation that they must follow that model to be a missionary-minded church. Rather, believers in the local assembly carry their witness to the nations by the power of the Spirit and their personal enthusiasm and vision. Evangelism and church planting are done in ways that the local assembly can handle, with its unique structure and support (1 Thess. 1:5–7; 2 Cor. 4:1–4).

Some are reluctant to emphasize the missional aspect of church when the new church plant is small and financially weak. They may assert that to emphasize mission will insult new believers and be a barrier to outreach. Other church planters may think that the congregation must mature in all other areas of Christian life and program before the mission focus is introduced. These arguments, however, do not conform to the pattern of the early church, in which people were not hindered by the congregation's age or vocabulary; the assemblies did all they could to get the Message to those in need, in all cultures within their reach. The early church grew by leaps and bounds because mission was a part of believing from the start. Believers, young and old, became active in every aspect of the church's total mission, in addition to that of their local assembly.

Four New Testament principles when applied to evangelism will enhance the spontaneous growth of the church.

1. Each one teaches one

New followers must learn at the outset that they have been empowered by the Holy Spirit to share what Jesus has done for them with their non-Christian friends. The Christian faith is a personal faith. This new birth principle will cause more to come to faith in Christ than any organized program can produce. The pioneer missiologist, Donald McGavran, writes, "It is the evangelist's main task to trust, to love, and to connect where he can."[5] Every believer becomes a partner in the process of telling others about Christ's power in daily living.

As with other aspects of worship, we must teach believers the ways of sharing their faith that are natural to their cultural patterns. Nonliterate believers could learn to use a simple picture as a teaching tool to share the Story with others. Memorizing a basic Scripture plan will enable others to share their faith. We must empower each convert to do what their setting permits them to do effectively, without overburdening them with unnecessary doctrinal weight. Reserve the complex "gospel road" methods to present Christ to those who will understand and appreciate lengthy explanations.

Let us avoid giving the impression that evangelism is for the livelihood of the movement. Talk about Jesus rather than the denomination or assembly. In his story of reaching Korea during and after the Korean War, Arch Campbell attests that

> Of the million that have come to the Savior and received Him ... nearly all have heard the good news from the lips of their own countrymen. The story goes from mouth to mouth and from heart to heart.[6]

2. Seek teachable moments

Help new followers learn to be sensitive to the social and spiritual needs of their neighbors. Teach them to pray for and seek those who are more receptive to the gospel. Help them discern moments of receptivity when their friends are ready to learn. Sharing one's faith needs to be a natural day-to-day part of life rather than a boxed-in method. We must model the attitude of being prepared to share the personal hope with people who ask, showing that all believers have a personal Story to tell about Christ in day-to-day events.

3. Connect through natural networks

Teach believers to share their newfound faith with those whom they already know, those who will watch them and who are also seeking the Truth. In his groundbreaking book, *The Bridges of God,* McGavran emphasized that every believer shares the Truth of Christ through family connections and natural contacts. Family leaders need to seek ways to pray with their own nuclear family members, sharing the Truth with them. The family network will also provide a safety net for believers in time of persecution. It is important that the new convert, like the mature follower, develop and maintain friendship contacts with non-believing relatives and friends. In most cases, sharing the faith with them will come more easily. Using family connections to share faith is a way to avoid the usual mission method of extracting new believers from their social connections, which hinders natural networking, stops growth, and leads to an inward-focus for self-preservation.

4. Pray for and connect through divine encounters

Teach believers to pray for encounters prepared by the Holy Spirit where they can share their faith in a natural setting, just when friends suddenly discover a personal spiritual need. The Holy Spirit offers many such revelations to people who are anchored in religious darkness. A divine encounter will focus thoughts and motivate people to seek the Christian friend who can answer their questions. When a believer ties the Truth to the encounter, a seeker will experience an "aha!" revelation. He or she will then be open to receiving and learning.

In applying these four principles, we demonstrate the attitude of planting seeds of Truth. We will teach the new believers that the Truth of Christ should be spread as "the sower's seed" (Matt. 13:3–4) is spread on all soils or souls. This is not something that the new believers do in order to present a report of decisions made. Rather, each follower practices seed planting with his friends and family members as a lifestyle.

The Christian who needs to report conversion numbers may often leave the impression that spiritual life is measured by statistics. This can cause new believers to focus on results rather than seeking to become more like Christ. Being numbers-driven may also lead the evangelist to force people to make a decision before it is time. As a result, those who come to Christ make superficial decisions and often don't count the cost of following Jesus.

The New Testament church had to face Gnostic beliefs, the Pharisees' legalism, and the cultural religion of Rome. Jude challenged them to "contend for the faith" that is unstained by falsehood (Jude 3). When someone claimed the Truth of Christ, they were also willing to contend for the faith. The story of the growth of Christian belief in China during Mao's revolution provides hundreds of stories that concur with *claiming the faith to keep it alive.* Once the Chinese believers realized that the belief of the "foreign devil" was truly valid even for them, they were willing to die for it. And many did die for this Truth! The fact that the Communist agenda to annihilate faith in Christ did not succeed is a testimony to the power of Christ. Jesus continues to keep his promise for His Church that even "the gates of Hell cannot overrun it" (Matt. 16:18).

The need to fight and protect the faith is a pressing one in the twenty-first century. The present smorgasbord of cults and shady teaching motivates us to contend for the faith through biblical worship and witness. When we develop Christ-focused worship and witness that belong to the follower, we will cultivate habits that believers can hold to and that will penetrate deeply into the heart of the culture. Church planters can then move on without fear that they have abandoned their calling. In reality, when the church is planted and taken by its believers, everyone wins!

Chapter 8

The Crisis of Leadership

Empower leaders who serve Christ

THE LONGEVITY OF the local church depends on a continuing cycle of empowering men and women to serve Christ and to reproduce their passion in others. Equipped leaders build powerful congregations. If you want the congregation you establish to outlive you, you will train leaders. As you pursue the qualities of a Christ-focused church, you will inculcate the values of a teaching-training and leading-serving model. As the church pursues these qualities, faith will become a feature of the culture.

A Letter from China

Motivated by his passion for teaching God's Truth, a listener wrote this letter to Trans World Radio. He reminds us of the importance of providing culturally appropriate methods of training workers who area able to serve in their context.

There is a major persecution for the sake of the gospel. Many house churches, some numbered to be over 500 people, are forced to stop meeting together. Now all ministers must hold proper licenses and churches must be registered at the Religious Affairs Bureau. But since I do not hold any Registration paper, I could do nothing but see our few hundred flocks being shut out from the door of our church. Seeing this situation, my heart burns like ants over a hot plate. Initially, I wanted to study in a seminary in Mainland China. Unfortunately, in China, only those with a high education level are qualified to apply for the seminaries' entrance examination. Hence, I am cut off from the hope of theological education. Yet, I am so thankful to God for your radio station that has the program, "Seminary of the Air." Now I can obtain theological education and be equipped to be a worker of God. Hallelujah![1]

When a person decides to follow Christ, he or she wants to learn more about Him. New believers have a constant hunger for God's Word, and when the church provides ways to fill that hunger, the future is insured. Spontaneous growth is best confirmed when sent-ones inculcate biblical values that are free of the sending church's cultural traits. We must understand these in the cultural context of the New Testament as we attempt to apply the biblical principle. When properly modeled through its leadership, the newly planted congregation will learn to adapt New Testament qualities and biblical concepts to their culture and will grow deeper in faith as a result.

Teaching-Training

The first believers were immediately brought into the teaching of the apostles because discipling new believers held high priority in the early church. And so it should be for emerging churches in the twenty-first century. A teaching-training church is one whose believers are always in a process of spiritual growth as they mature in their knowledge of Christ, just as they received Him (Col. 2:6–7). As their gifts and capabilities emerge in the assembly, leaders are trained, mentored in the attitudes of service, and educated in the Scripture so that they become approved leaders.[2] The importance of training should not surprise us, especially when we remember that Great Commission recorded in Matthew 28 places primary emphasis on making disciples.

The church planting team must incorporate training into their program at two levels or tracks. The first track, *discipling believers*, aims at bringing every believer "to the maturity of the stature which belongs to the fullness of Christ" (Eph. 4:13b). The second track, *training leaders*, aims at leading selected believers to exercise their gifts as apostles, prophets, evangelists, pastors, and teachers so that they will "equip the saints for the work of service, to the building of the body of Christ" (Eph. 4:11–12).

1. Discipling the believers

Discipling the followers can be done through a variety of methods or teaching formats. The way you nurture new believers and the methods by which you train leaders will affect spontaneous growth of the church.

Teaching new believers is the primary responsibility of the church planter. Although the term *teaching* speaks of the whole process of Christian growth, from new birth to maturity in service, I will limit its definition in this section to describe the process of training and shepherding believers to maturity in the knowledge of Christ. Paul described how the result of equipping the saints means they are "no longer to be children, tossed here and there by waves, and carried about by every wind of doctrine, by the trickery of men, by craftiness in deceitful scheming; but speaking the truth in love, we are to grow up in all aspects into Him ... being fitted and held together ..." (Eph. 4:14–16). Every person who holds to the name of Christ must become involved in this process.

Maturing the believers should adhere to three basic presuppositions in order to build the church within the cultural context.

A. Disciple all believers of all ages. Aim to bring all to maturity, within the capability of the individual's level of maturity. This means you will need to develop an environment of "growing in Christ" with all believers—men, women, youth, and children—from the moment a person trusts Christ. This understanding should be so commonly held by Christians that any new follower will recognize the expectation for maturing and immediately become involved in the group process.

Some cultures hinder this presupposition because they underestimate the ability of children to learn. Others don't want girls to be taught because they fear that education might make them proud and insubordinate. Some cultures will not allow women to acquire knowledge, as that might threaten their husband's status. All cultural hindrances to spiritual maturity need to be overcome through biblical teaching and modeling that places value on everyone being able to learn God's Truth.

B. Empower the believer for ministry. Direct the believer toward service and outreach. The maturing process should move from learning the biblical Truth to immediate application. Whether the lesson being taught is about prayer, giving, trust, or obedience, the believer should see how it works in everyday life. In this way, the Truth will transform life and motivate Christians to share their belief with others. As they are empowered to live out their faith in service, natural leaders will emerge for further training.

C. Use a variety of training formats. Seek to train believers in a context that fits their environment. This requires setting up teaching formats that are conducive to learning. These formats should be such that the believers can easily accept. I will suggest five general types of teaching forms that help believers mature in Christ.

First, disciple believers in *small groups.* As a person comes to Christ, he should be integrated into a fellowship with familiar faces. This will encourage regular attendance, and it will enable mature Christians to follow up on the newcomer and keep him accountable. Small groups can be formed around family clusters, geographic proximity, age, work identity, or other areas of similarity. There should be some factor that gives the participants a sense of cohesion or belonging.

The leader or group may choose the content or curriculum to be studied. Subject material may be selected from the corps of leaders of the larger assembly, or leaders must be taught to choose biblical topics according to the group's need. The teaching-elder is accountable to a spiritual mentor, which helps give direction and maintain biblical correctness in teaching and worship within the groups. Small groups must periodically participate in a large group celebration, as this is a reminder of the Truth of the visible, universal Church. Multi-group celebrations will also help the believers to identify with the Body of Christ that is larger than their own.

Second, disciple believers by *shepherding individuals.* One-on-one training and modeling deepens the new follower's obedience. This process is especially helpful with baby Christians who need individual attention from a more mature disciple of Christ. Shepherding can be done one-to-one, woman-to-woman, man-to-man, or teen-to-teen. Through this mentoring relationship, the new Christian can more easily get assimilated into the cell group and the larger assembly.

Third, disciple believers in *corporate worship*. This is more easily facilitated in countries where there is social or political freedom to meet in public assemblies. But even in places where the laws or dominant religion prohibit such gatherings, there may be opportunities for big groups to assemble. This enhances a sense of belonging to the Body of Christ, thus modeling the Truth of the universal Church, and reduces feelings of isolation or being forgotten.

Fourth, disciple believers through *cultural learning events*. Use occasions for which the society in general comes together for holidays, festivals, and other events. For example, most cultures have their rites of passage, but some cultures place higher emphasis on a person's passage from one age group to another and will have an initiation ceremony or a celebration to mark the occasion. Believers can plan "faith rites of passage" as developmental stages of Christian maturing that will serve to disciple people in practical holiness and responsibility.

For example, some people groups in India and West Africa practice a ceremony marking the teen's transition to adulthood during which the young adult is taught the wisdom of the ancestors. At the end of this period the initiates must perform certain dances before the clan to show that they have successfully passed from childhood to adulthood. Some groups even name this event "new birth" or "new beginnings." Followers of Christ in this culture could easily develop a similar ceremony of "new birth" for Christians who have fulfilled the requirements for baptism as the final testimony of passage to Christian maturity.

In similar ways, women should be mentored in their role as trainers of children. Teach them in their homes and in more formal settings about childcare, hygiene, discipline, and teaching children Scripture. Men's groups can be formed to challenge men to remain strong in their faith, to lead their family in worship and living, to make a difference in society by training their children, and to be accountable to one another. Teens can learn how to live a holy life among their peers. Their enthusiasm for peer activity can be harnessed to bring them together during short school breaks, if they are in school, or at appropriate seasons to teach them subjects relevant to their needs. John and Isobel Kuhn of the China Inland Mission, now known as Overseas Mission Fellowship, describe the varieties of one month-long school for the Lisu people of Western China.[3] Separate programs were held for church leaders, cowherds, teenagers, and young children. These programs were fitted into the rural activities of the people, enabling them to attend at a time of the year most suited to their environment, social class, and farming cycle.

2. Training leaders

This second track flows naturally out of discipling believers. Although a limited number of persons will become group leaders, the process of leadership training begins with conversion. New followers learn from the outset that they are leaders in their world of influence. They must be taught how to live and lead as people of God.

The New Testament teaches of the need for various levels of leaders, whose combined ministries enhance church growth. Apostles have a broad, outreaching ministry, and evangelists specifically serve the rebirthing need of the Body. Deacons, elders, and pastor-teachers build up the local parish or congregation, and teachers influence the intellectual maturing of the Body. Bishops oversee differing sizes of groups (Eph. 4:11–12; 1 Tim. 3:1 –6; Titus 1:5–9).

In the emerging assembly, the selection of leaders for the various ministries should rise from natural patterns of leading in the micro-congregation of the family. Therefore, the future decision makers should first be trained to give spiritual leadership in their families. They should be taught how to lead family prayer, Bible teaching, and other worship events. A church planter may have to take time to demonstrate this leadership role in the new believer's home. An informal accountability process must to be set up whereby the leaders are encouraged as they report about what God has been doing in their families. As a person matures in this first sphere of influence, his leadership potential will be evident to the larger assembly.

All Christians must be encouraged to see themselves as spiritual leaders by emphasizing that we are each called to serve in our world. This helps avoid competition, and it develops spiritual elders according to the cultural meaning of that duty, within the biblical parameters. Some cultures lean heavily on formally educated clergy; others are satisfied with an informal, less academic approach.

The most effective format for developing leaders is an informal mentoring process in which the more spiritually mature person spends time with the emerging leader, helping him or her develop spiritual skills and to grow in the knowledge of Christ. As this training orients believers to ministry, they can be taught how to use their leadership aptitude to serve their people.

We must be careful not to create an educational expectation in leadership training that gives birth to a clergy-laity dichotomy. The traditional residential training schools tend to take people out of their social setting to train them as pastors and church leaders. This method is often expensive and time-consuming, resulting in the formation of people who see themselves as a cut above their Christian peers.

If, however, a formal educational program is essential to the future of the church movement, there are four helpful guidelines that will limit overpriced leadership training, and that insure that the leaders-in-training will remain in touch with their Church of origin.

A. The local believers choose the leader for their assembly. Each culture has its intrinsic values associated with leadership, values that the outsider will not often understand. Some missionaries have made the mistake of choosing a promising young prospect for a position of leadership. Unfortunately, some prospects look promising only to the foreigner, but the hosts do not see them in the same light. Christians should be encouraged to choose for themselves those who are potential or real leaders. The sent-one must consistently teach people the qualities of holiness, putting before the people the image of godliness that will guide them when choosing a leader.

Selecting only younger men and women for leadership training is dangerous, especially if the candidates have not previously proven their calling or leadership capability. Knowledge is power, and knowledge-power can corrupt those who lack the wisdom or social position that the culture expects them to have in order to lead. If a young leader is trained when the congregation or culture prefers older people, he may not be given full freedom to serve because his knowledge is seen as a threat to the social status of his seniors. Consequently, his leadership will hinder church growth.

B. The believers support their candidate. The local assembly chooses the candidates for special training because they deem them capable of leading. The assembly and not the foreigner should bear the financial burden for training, so that leaders feel the support of their own people and set their allegiance to them, not to the foreigner. This will also help them be more motivated to serve their people upon completion of their training.

C. The believers choose training that is culturally relevant to their assembly. Leadership development should use training models that match the local church's need. A training program should be selected keeping in mind four important pedagogical principles that guide this kind of learning process.

First, the *curriculum* should be appropriate and useful to the need of the church. The foreign worker who hastily transfers his culture's model of theological education often forgets that it may not be relevant to the local church's culture. Therefore, the missionary and his team should not present their hosts with a predetermined curriculum. Careful evaluation of the culture will inform them of the teaching methods and content that will be most appropriate for the leader-trainee.

Second, the pedagogical presupposition of the training school and the curriculum should emphasize *practical application of God's Truth to local ministry.* The New Testament demonstrates a pattern that I believe is basic to every culture's learning style: Christians *did* ministry. Out of *doing* came the awareness of a need for more knowledge (Acts 6:1–7; 8:4; 17:24–28; 20:17; Rom. 16:3, 12). This knowledge was sought through prayer and Bible study, always carried out under the tutorship of a mentor. As a consequence, the leader-in-training learned *with* his experience.

The leaders of the New Testament church did not see themselves as superior to others because the experience and the mentoring relationship always reminded them, either consciously or subconsciously, that there was always more to learn. In the final analysis, the leader-trainee quickly owned the knowledge because it worked in his life-experience—it was knowledge in practice. This is the model we should seek in training leaders for the church of Christ.

The prevailing pattern used in contemporary leadership training should be evaluated in light of this principle. The commonly used approach, whereby we first impart a large quantity of knowledge and then require praxis, may not be the best way to train. It sometimes causes young leaders to feel superior to the elders because of their greater knowledge. This false assumption may also exaggerate the distinction between the clergy and the laity. Ultimately, spontaneous growth is hindered.

Third, *lessons must be taught in the language of ministry*. The student should learn in the language that he would be using in ministry. The Bible or New Testament should also be provided in the native language of the student. If these texts are not available, then lesson plans should provide the biblical material in the language for that person or class group. In some cases, many vernacular languages will be represented in the training session, which will require the use of a commonly understood language of instruction. Even if the vehicle of communication is not the heart language, the teaching must encourage each student to transform the material into his or her mother tongue. That way, the trainees will be less inclined to use the educational language as a tool to prove that they are highly educated. The language of instruction and the learning environment will either encourage or discourage an attitude of superiority. It is important that students graduate from the training school with a deep desire to communicate with their people in a manner that is understandable and acceptable.

The fourth principle of contextual leadership training expects that *the location of the training program will be as close as possible to the context of future ministry*. The more the learner remains attached to his home culture, the more quickly will he apply his knowledge to service. Mission organizations have often worked on the assumption that separation from one's people or home environment helps the learner concentrate on his lessons. As a result, some have built large colleges and expensive schools away from the future ministry setting. Although impressive, these campuses often burden the church with locally unaffordable education. Furthermore, expensive and distant schools sometimes disassociate the student from his people, and reverse culture shock often retards the graduate's readjustment to his home ministry setting.

The contextual leadership-training program should be affordable for the student and for the sending congregation. Planners should choose the location, curriculum, and the length of time within reach of the supporting congregation's financial resources. High cost of training will prohibit some congregations from sending good candidates. In some situations, locally available and affordable education may mean that the traditional resident Bible school is not the best choice.

Non-residential training—training in which the students do not reside on a campus—is flexible and able to adapt to many different models. When it is better for the student to remain at home, we must keep in mind that theological education by extension is only one vehicle of training that keeps the learner in the home setting. Other models such as month-long or short-term vernacular schools or periodic modular classes can be equally effective. In all cases, the education must be fashioned to the local culture and its needs.

D. The believers may send some candidates abroad for higher education, but they must plan carefully. Although locally operated and affordable leadership training is preferred, there may be a special need for superior education. The candidate and the sending congregation should follow the principles mentioned in this section, giving special attention to four additional criteria.

First, *the candidate choice must be based on objective criteria.* These include academic ability, personal character, and long-term commitment to the emerging church. These requirements must be written and understood by all parties involved before the selection process begins. Every effort should be made to avoid basing selection on racial or family qualifications.

Second, *the congregation must commit to the long-term financial burden* of this training. If necessary, the senders should seek out additional scholarship funds. If the congregation raises more of the funding than the missionary or mission organization, the student's accountability to his people is enhanced. As a result of the financial outlay for education, the church may ask the trainee to make a formal commitment to serve them after graduation.

Third, *the candidate's immediate family should accompany him* on the study leave. The wife should also be trained, using a curriculum that meets her needs and academic level, as this will increase the couple's chances of success in training as well as future ministry. It will strengthen their marriage as they begin to understand how to serve together, and temper potential accusations of either spouse's unfaithfulness that may come later in their life of ministry.

Fourth, every step possible must be taken to *keep the student connected with home*. Students should be kept accountable to the home church by sending regular reports, grades, and newsletters. When the trainee returns, the local congregation must assign him to his new post. The foreign missionary or mission team should not appoint the returnee to ministry, lest this give the impression that the mission team owns the new pastor.

Teaching and training enhance the spontaneous growth of the emerging church. As they grow in their faith, all believers must see themselves as an integral part of the whole process of maturing. The description we have seen of the teaching-training church does not propose that a certain method of model is best for a given culture, but it requires that what is done will edify the believers and enhance their focus on Christ in their environment.

Leading-Serving

A leading-serving church is a community of believers who respond to one another's needs, as they respond to Christ who is the Head of the Church (Eph. 5:23). The Holy Spirit has distributed among this Body administrative, serving, ruling, and other gifts (Rom. 12; 1 Cor. 12; Eph. 4:11–12), and everyone is to serve knowing that they are accountable to the Head (Eph. 5:24). Those appointed to shepherd the flock must do so according to the will of God, not lording it over others but displaying such a spirit of service that the younger believers willingly submit to them (1 Pet. 5:1–6). Every believer is accountable to the spiritual authority that has been established by God through the believing community.

Both leaders and followers must discipline themselves according to the ethics of Scripture (Eph. 5–6; Col. 3–4; 1 Pet. 2:1–17). The believers submit to correction, in keeping with the biblical injunction to guard their holiness (Matt. 18:15–20; 1 Cor. 5:1–8; Gal. 6:1–5; Jude 20–24). The leaders demonstrate, by their character, how followers of Christ maintain order and decorum in worship and ministry (1 Cor. 14:33, 40). This will help keep the unity and peace of Christ among the members of His Body (Titus 3:8–11; Eph. 4:1–5).

The early church organized its leadership structure around elders, deacons, and apostles, and Paul would describe the role of the overseer as a noble task (1 Tim. 3:1). This church was forced by persecution and social change to remain flexible in its organization, but the leaders maintained order and discipline in the assembly. Frequently, believers were instructed in their manner of discipline. Jesus had given a step-by-step approach for dealing with an errant one (Matt.18:15–20), and the apostles spoke to this issue as well. Paul asked those who were spiritual to restore sinners "in the spirit of gentleness" (Gal. 6:1). In extreme cases, he instructed that the sinner be delivered to Satan "for the destruction of his flesh, that his spirit may be saved" (1 Cor. 5:5)

As church planters, we should guide the development of a leading-serving church according to three principles.

1. Enable leaders to mature to their level of competence

I previously stressed the importance of leadership development as a natural part of the training and maturing process in the life of the assembly. The sent-one helps new believers to understand the biblical expectations and ethics to which leaders must adhere in order to develop the internal quality of a servant rather than the external, politicized concept that is often corrupted by human nature. Even the manner in which the assembly selects upper level leaders and administrators should not focus on power; rather it should create an atmosphere of servanthood. This downplays a focus on authority and structure, and averts what could become a race for the presidency. It also prevents elevating people to a position for which they are incompetent, for every leader should fulfill the needs of the congregation at his level of competence.

2. Enable the believers to organize their structure

The Christ-focused congregation that is beginning to mature determines its own organization as the local believers start applying biblical principles of leadership to their context. (Examples of this can be found in Acts 6:1–7, 15:1–21, and 20:13–38.) The foreign worker will come to the host culture with his cultural methods of administration in mind, instinctively believing that this way of running a church is correct. The tendency will be to apply this structure to the new context, but the temptation to do this must be resisted. If you are a church planter serving in a culture where the church has not yet taken root, don't plan an organizational structure before the believers are gathered. Instead, encourage the new church to organize a culturally relevant structure of its own, allow the organization to emerge from within the fellowship, and help the new believers set patterns that fit the Scripture within the local context.

As the believers are gathered and discipled, they will come with impressions of how their work should function. As they formulate their concepts of structure in keeping with biblical guidelines, the organization will respond and correspond to the demands of the congregation and their culture. They should be empowered through the training process to follow biblical principles as they make decisions and solve problems. This means giving instructions, modeling, and then stepping aside. In some cases, if the church is planted in a culture where Christianity already exists, the new believers may already have notions of church organization. The sent-one can guide them through the biblical and cultural meanings of leadership and organization so that they develop a structure that is functional, one that keeps people focused on serving Christ and one another, not the organization.

3. Teach congregations to look *first* to the Bible in matters of discipline and order

Foster the conviction that the Scriptures provide all that is necessary so "that the man of God may be adequate, equipped for every good work" (2 Tim. 3:17). Help the new believers to understand the holiness and justice of God, and how He is always working with them to conform them to the image of His Son (Rom. 8:29). Teach them the scriptural principles for church discipline and order, but allow them to figure out how the principles work. The organization and discipline of the emerging church must flow with the people it encircles. It must help the church grow deeper into the image of Christ, while causing the church's influence to penetrate further into society. The foreign worker must not assume the role of the disciplinarian. Instead, he or she must help the assembly to understand the application of Scripture to their culture, allowing them to respond to the Holy Spirit and develop their biblically-based disciplinary process.

Note that this description of the leading-serving church does not preclude or presuppose a certain governmental form that must be applied to the assembly. Rather, the emerging congregation determines its structure and applies the disciplinary approach that is valid to their context, yet true to the values of Scripture. In the evaluation tool in Appendix B, the characteristics attributed to the teaching-training and leading-serving criteria do not describe programs or financially supported events. Rather, the focus is on biblical attitudes and actions that the Christ-centered church incorporates into their life. These are culturally transferable and enhance spontaneous growth because they are qualities that the believers can hold as their own.

In summary, the Christ-centered church is not defined by an outside culture unless that distant assembly happens to be the biblical model. Make every effort to transfer the biblical value of the church without succumbing to your cultural biases, and trust the Holy Spirit to guide the new believers to a ministry style that works in their culture and that does not violate the Scriptures. Lead the emerging congregation to discover its cultural equivalent of the Body of Christ that resides in the local community.

William Smalley aptly described this kind of church in his definition of the indigenous church. According to him,

> It is a group of believers who live out their life, including their socialized Christian activity, in the patterns of the local society, and for whom any transformation of that society comes out of their felt needs under the guidance of the Holy Spirit and the Scripture.[4]

This kind of church, however, does not come into being without someone giving the believers the direction and input necessary to empower them in their spiritual maturing. As a model of leadership, the sent-one must teach the Scripture and help people understand their own culture instead of thrusting upon them the model of his home church, which is culture-bound. Our goal is to develop a church that affects its culture to the level that the early believers changed theirs.

Smalley rightly stated that we must see the Bible in its cultural context, and see God working within the host culture. According to him, our responsibility is "to lead them in prayer to find what God would have them to do as they study His Word and seek the interpretation and leadership of the Holy Spirit."[5]

Trained People Become a Sending Congregation[6]

A young church had quickly grown to over a hundred worshipers, but its pastor had a global vision. He felt called to plant a new congregation in a town 250 kilometers away, and he wanted his assembly to become part of this courageous step, which would mean his eventual relocation to the distant town. How would he lay the groundwork for a move that some would see as a divided allegiance?

The pastor trained his leaders to pray for a larger vision and he developed shepherding groups. He trained people in leading and caring for one another. At the same time, he continued to implant a global vision within the congregation. As they prayed and planned, they watched the Lord open new opportunities for ministry. The day finally came when the pastor and his family moved to the new city, tearfully sent off by their congregation. In the absence of the pastor, the elders preached, counseled, and encouraged the believers who were excited to experience the impact of their faith in action both at home and in the other city. As a result, new people outside their fellowship began to inquire about the obvious excitement and engaged themselves with these dynamic people.

When people are trained to lead with what they hold in their hands, their faith gives energy to a spontaneous movement. But if the assembly must depend on another group, then neither the worship nor the witness, leading, teaching, or mission efforts belong to them. Personal faith is a stranger in their house, because it is not a faith that expresses *their* values. That is why spontaneous growth depends on the believers possessing and being possessed by Christ. As a sent-one who declares Christ in order to establish the church in unreached areas, you must focus their attention on the One who is the Way, the Truth, and the Life. Ultimately, He is the One who will take them through difficult times.

Chapter 9

The Crisis of Relationships with the Church

Pursue harmony in your relationship with the emerging church

THE WORLD WANTS to see unity. People feel comfortable when they know that there is oneness and peace. The problem in missions, however, is that unexpected tension springs to life when the sent-one lives and works in a new culture, where local believers want to do things their way. They want to make their own decisions. The foreigner might work with a national pastor who has different values about money or applies church discipline differently. Or he might have to take orders from a local director whose leadership paradigm is not like his own.

The era of multinational team partnerships has thrust many workers into undesirable conflicts. For example, a sent-one was assigned to work with a local church to develop their outreach to a Hindu people group. The agreement between mission leaders and the national church was promising, but as the foreign worker interacted with the local believers he discovered that the Christians had no desire to serve Hindus. The Christians thought of these people as a menace, belonging to a caste for which there was no hope of Christian conversion. The more the missionary tried to pursue his goals of outreach to the Hindus, the more inflamed were the reactions from his national counterparts. If the missionary and local leaders could not find a solution, the former would have to return home. How could this be solved?

The crisis in this chapter concerns our working relationship with Christians and churches of another culture. This study will help you more if you take time to assess your perspective. A right attitude will enhance your effort to work through differences of opinion with workers who are also seeking to bring the Message to neighbors who need to experience Christ's love.

Our Common Point of Agreement

The Bible teaches everything we need to know about relationships in the church, the *ekklesia*. It defines who we are as the chosen people of God, thereby clarifying the nature and the role of the sent-one. From this base, we can develop missiological principles that describe how a foreign worker is to relate to the church in the host's culture.

1. The church is an assembly of chosen people

The church is people who adhere to the same conviction about Christ, but the idea of "church" as a people is often confused with "church" as an organization. Church history and world politics have not always understood the difference between the church and the visible institution, causing many to wrongly view the church as an organization having secular power. We must understand the nature of the church and how that applies to the crises among its foreign and local leaders.

A. The church is a special people. The people who make up the church are redeemed by the blood of Jesus (Eph. 1:7), called and set apart (Rom. 1:6–7; 8:28), sent out into the world (Matt. 28:19; John 20:21), and transformed by the Holy Spirit's power (2 Cor. 3:18). This is true of each and all churches, regardless of race (Col. 3:11).

B. The church is a serving people. The church is composed of people who respond to the needs of their community and are willing to serve their neighbors (Acts 6:1–6). They have not become so otherworldly that they can no longer relate to this environment. They are people who pray (Acts 12:12), and who persevere in the face of impending danger (Acts 5:33–42). They are a witnessing body (John 15:26–27; Acts 1:8). They minister to one another's needs (Rom 12; 1 Cor 12–14), worship together (Acts 2:42–47), and are generous with their wealth (Acts 4:32–35; 2 Cor. 8–9).

C. The church is a people who form the Body of Christ. These redeemed and set-apart people belong to one universal if unseen organism called "the Body of Christ" (Rom. 12:5; 1 Cor. 12:27; Eph. 1:22–23; 5:23; Col. 1:18). As such, the believers of different assemblies are interrelated through a common bond of knowing Christ. The Holy Spirit has placed each one into Christ's Body (1 Cor. 12:13), and each is subject to Jesus, who is the Head of the Body (Eph. 5:23). They all have equal status under their Head.

This means that both the sending church and the planted church compose the universal Body of Christ. The former provided the sending agency or mission organization, and released its sent-ones to establish the church in the host country. The sent-ones must be convinced that the local assembly is just as much the church as their home congregation, for the self-image of both is anchored in seeing Christ as their Head.

2. The foreign worker is a sent-one

The word "missionary" comes from the Latin word meaning "sent-one," and a missionary is the apostle (*apostolos*) of the twenty-first century. The term is seen as passé, even undesirable, to some. Others have diluted its meaning by teaching that everyone is a missionary, and while I can understand their good intentions, the early church used the term specifically. They defined the worker's role as a sent-one (missionary) whenever a congregation or church society *sent* one of its members to serve in another culture for the purpose of enhancing or sharing the Message. Five qualities make the worker a sent-one.

A. The foreign worker is an ambassador, sent with the purpose of taking the Message of reconciliation in Christ to a shattered world (2 Cor. 5:20). He is a part of the Body of Christ in a local assembly, but chosen and sent to establish a local assembly of the Body in another location, which is also composed of those who have been baptized into Christ as members of His Body.

B. The sent-one is set apart and released to go from the sending church. Paul was set apart with Barnabas by the church in Antioch (Acts 13:1–6) and were accountable through that church's commission to fulfill their duty as sent-ones (Acts 14:26–28). They were under the authority of that church to complete the task (Acts 15:30–35), and responsible to send back reports to them (Acts 14:27). These expectations equally apply to believers in the planted church, when one of them is sent by his assembly to establish the church among another people.

C. The sent-one is part of a larger whole. The missionary is not the sum total of the gifts and capabilities in the local church. Paul saw himself as the planter but recognized that others also played important roles in fulfilling the work of the kingdom of God (1 Cor. 3:4–9). He saw the spiritual life of the church as primarily the responsibility of individual believers within the local assembly and therefore encouraged and taught new believers to be obedient to the Spirit (Eph. 5:1–2, 18). As the temple of the Holy Spirit (1 Cor. 6:19), each one was valuable and responsible.

D. The sent-one advises as a participant, but he cannot mandate. The missionary is an outsider in that he is not an integral part of the local culture in the same way as the local believer is an insider. Paul refused to lord it over the believers but instead encouraged them to stand firm in the faith (2 Cor. 1:23–24). He certainly spoke with the authority he had as an apostle, but he refrained from wielding it wrongly. He used the approach of teaching through letters, to advise and direct where there was clear divergence from holy behavior (1 Cor. 5). This was in keeping with his authority as the spiritual father of the assembly, but it was always the local believers who had to make corrections. The foreign worker may have insight into spiritual problems on the basis of his experience, but once he has established a local assembly of believers, he takes on the role of a teacher of Scripture, and that with some degree of separation.

E. The sent-one serves a temporary role in the local assembly. The missionary establishes the local assembly, helps the believers set up their leadership structure according to their culture and needs, and then moves on to repeat the process elsewhere. Paul spent two Sabbath days at Pisidian Antioch (Acts 13:14, 44), a "long time" at Iconium (14:3), and days in the region of Derbe and Lystra (14:21, 23). He spent "some days" in Philippi (16:12), three Sabbaths in Thessalonica (17:2), a year and six months at Corinth (18:11), and two years in Ephesus (19:10). In most of these places, Paul was forced by political or social conditions to leave, but in each place he served long enough to plant a viable assembly of believers. Ultimately, it was the local congregation that had to assume the primary role in its own survival.

Defining the Relationship

The example of Paul helps us to draw seven missiological conclusions about the nature of the inter-relationship between the sent-one and the emerging church.[1]

1. A micro-image of the larger Body

Every local assembly of believers is an expression of the larger Body of Christ. This assembly must look to Christ in obedience and for guidance just as the church planter does or did. No one church, including the sending church, is a greater or lesser model of the Body.

2. Unity in diversity

There is unity within the diversity of groups. Although we celebrate cultural diversity, we recognize that oneness comes through knowing Christ as Savior and Lord. In every assembly, belief and obedience to Christ are nurtured through teaching, worship, and the like.

3. Unique expression

Each assembly expresses its unique social or cultural nature through worship and service. This does not place one congregation above another in spirituality or truth, so long as each expresses its nature under the authority of Christ, the Head. Just because one has more money or greater programs does not mean that it is a better example of the church. No assembly should be set up as a model of a good church. Instead, each assembly should evaluate its own maturing against the model of Scripture and the knowledge of Christ. The Apostle Paul made only one comparative statement in his letters about the church he planted (2 Cor. 8:1), and this was not intended to create a competitive spirit but to test the sincerity of the Corinthian church (v. 8).

4. Biblical discipline

The local assembly disciplines the errant member according to biblical principles as they apply to the local culture. The methods and logic for arriving at a disciplinary procedure will be colored by culture but always guided by Scripture.

5. Bible-centered autonomy

Each assembly is free from other assemblies to worship and walk in biblical holiness. It is the local assembly of believers that fulfills the biblical expression of the church in its culture, as each is led by the Holy Spirit and through obedience to the Scripture. The sent-one must not overrule or usurp the autonomous church nature of the emerging church. The mission organization cannot worship on behalf of the planted church. It cannot evangelize, teach, or administer the sacraments for the local believer, whether through manipulation, domination, or participation. The sent-one cannot be telling the planted assembly what to do. He cannot dominate the local expression of the Body of Christ, which he has established and nurtured to be obedient to the Holy Spirit.

6. Mobility

The sent-one remains free from attachment to the local assembly in order to move on to a new area. The local assembly cannot retain him as a permanent fixture but must instead be supportive of, and even participate in, the continuing ministry of the missionary to a new people.

7. Accountability

Both the local church and the missionary are equally accountable to God and to each other to complete the full expression of the adult church. Each allows the other to mature in the self-expression that ultimately glorifies God (Eph. 1:3–14; 4:11–16).

In conclusion, a congregation of God's people sends out someone who will establish another gathering of God's people. The sending group, the sent-one, and the emerging group are one because they are all in Christ, but the worker must remain accountable to his group of origin as he serves in a distant culture. David Hesselgrave concludes a brief essay on the biblical base for relationship with these words:

> It is evident that local churches today are not related to any other church in exactly the same way as those first-century churches were related to the Jerusalem church. Churches today do not have a mother church in that sense. But today's churches are

authentic churches only to the extent that they evidence subjection to the same apostolic authority by adhering to the faith and practice of the Holy Scriptures. It is this adherence that marks them as part of the Universal Church. Moreover, this adherence will lead to *koinonia* with other churches under the same authority—a *koinonia* that will find practical expression in cooperation in good works and glad witness.[2]

The Relationship of the Mission Team and the Emerging Church

The goal of every church planter is to leave behind a Christ-centered church that expresses its faith within its cultural context in a biblical manner. This church has been variously described as an indigenous church, an autonomous church, a mature church, an adult congregation, and a dynamic equivalent church. In chapter 6 we described the biblical nature of this church by calling it Christ-centered. The problem to be resolved, however, is for sent-ones to know how to relate to this local assembly. We will be helped in this endeavor by forming two important habits.

First, we must believe that this new assembly is the Church. As foreign workers, we must be convinced that the emerging national church is capable of demonstrating Christ-centered qualities. Although this sounds trite, our cultural values concerning church are very strong. Often, our ethnicity and the attachment to our country cause us to believe that our sending church is the true image of the Church of Jesus. This assumption may influence us to coach an assembly to imitate that image without realizing that it is culture-bound and may not be relevant to the host culture.

The emerging church must also learn to see itself as a local congregation that relates to other congregations, even though it is often easier for the sent-one and the local believers to see themselves as a branch of the mission agency. This false self-image will hinder local believers if they see themselves as unable to be a viable church when the missionary isn't around anymore. This is why we must ground the assembly's self-image in seeing Christ and not the sending agency as the final authority. Both sending church and local congregation are a national church within the universal Body of

Christ, and the national church that anchors its identity in Christ will more quickly take responsibility for its spiritual life.

Second, we must choose the appropriate relationship balance with the emerging church. Working together toward Christ-centeredness assumes that the sent-ones and the local believers have learned the same biblical values about themselves as the Church. Out of this foundational understanding comes the pattern for their relationship in ministry.

Two relationship images are commonly used to illustrate the relationship of the mission and the local church. While both have their merits, each enables us to understand aspects of this complex missiological problem.

A) The scaffold-skeleton comparison: Imagine a line with a skeleton at one end and a scaffold to the other, as shown in Figure 1.

A scaffold is a structure placed on the outside of a building under construction. This external structure is temporary, and it is removed when the building is completed. Using this analogy, a church planting team can enter the host country with a blueprint of the emerging church. We lead the new believers, developing them into a living organism called the Body of Christ, but our long-term vision is to move on to another site when this group is in place and express the presence of Christ in that new culture.

At the other extreme of the continuum is the skeleton. This is the internal frame that gives stability and function to the organism that is added onto its form. The human body has an internal bone structure, the skeleton, on which the flesh and muscle are attached. This gives force and purpose to the movement of the muscles and without it, the flesh is unable to function. Similarly, we enter the host culture aware that our presence and ministry are essential to the establishment and functioning of the emerging church. We provide the internal structure around which the new believers find their identity and being. We encourage a Christ-centered church to develop an infrastructure that is akin to that of its culture, while always being biblically accurate. The local believers are to express worship, discipline, training, and moral behavior in a culturally relevant manner. As the emerging church matures, we will naturally transition out of the skeleton and be replaced by trained local believers. Thus, when the internal design is functioning with locally trained believers, we move on and repeat the process among another people group. The one hindrance to moving on is that the sent-one may feel that local people cannot or will not do the same quality of ministry as he can. In such cases, we must remember that correctness or quality in functioning should be assessed according to the values and needs of the local culture, not according to the standards of our home culture.

Figure 1. Skeleton-Scaffold

Skeleton **Scaffold**

B) The fusion-dichotomy relationship: Once again, imagine the same continuum, with the idea of fusion at one extreme and that of dichotomy or separation at the other, as illustrated in Figure 2 below.

Figure 2. Fusion-Dichotomy

Fusion   **Modified Dichotomy**   **Dichotomy**

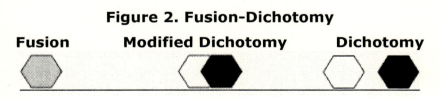

Fusion describes the action of two entities or bodies becoming one to the extent that neither is recognizable as it was in its former condition. Joined in one new body, each loses its former identity. We can partially compare fusion with marriage, where a man and a woman become one in the biblical sense. But just as a good marriage does not dissolve the distinctiveness of either partner, so too in the church-mission relationship, there is distinctiveness in character but oneness in essence. The fusion of the mission with the planted church is a union where the two become one. Family-oriented societies compare this to two families coming together through marriage. They live under the same roof, work in the same fields, and hold all things in common. One's success becomes everyone's joy, and one's failure becomes everyone's sorrow. Hence, in the fused mission-church relationship, the mission finances, including missionary salaries, go through the local church's organization, as do all decisions regarding the foreign worker. Pastors and church workers, whether foreign or national, are treated with equal esteem, having the same lines of accountability within church polity. A local believer could become a president of the national church as easily as an expatriate. This ecclesial form is similar to what some colonizing nations saw as the assimilation of one culture or politic into the other. A drawback of the colonial model, however, is that it often assumed that the ruling culture's values would swallow those of the subjugated culture, thereby making the latter advanced or civilized in the eyes of the former.

The demand to fuse the mission into the church arose in the early 1960s. Countries that had been colonized by Europe were gaining political independence, and this social-political attitude pushed national churches to seek control of their destiny. For example, Dr. Louis King, then foreign secretary of the Christian and Missionary Alliance, was faced with many pleas for independence, but including the request to let the missionary remain behind. Many national church leaders knew that they could not function well without the foreign presence but they wanted to lead *their* church. These demands came from good intentions, but lacked an understanding of the results of this fusion. Through his relationships with the mission leaders in the World Council of Churches (WCC), Dr. King was able to research the consequences of fusion with different mission boards. With the help of his friends, Dr. King accessed approximately sixty case studies of groups that had chosen fusion. He stated that "in every case it proved to be a disaster for the mission."[3] Often, it was only a few months before the foreign workers returned home, discouraged with their ministry experience. They had lost their sense of purpose as sent-ones and became what Dr. King called "a lackey of the church."

Dichotomy, at the other extreme of the fusion-dichotomy continuum, speaks of dividing into two separate forms. For example, a dichotomous tree is one that has two seed forms in the same pod. In missions this term refers to a relationship in which the two groups remain separate entities, often working completely apart from the other. Each retains the distinctiveness of its character and function, often without need to confer with the other. The principle can be illustrated as two families that live in the same village. Each family works in its own field. They empathize and confer with one another, and they help each another, but each maintains its separateness. In mission, this dichotomy includes, on one side, the emerging church denomination, which has authority over all the aspects of its churches, and the foreign mission or sending agency on the other side. A committee between the two groups might coordinate activities, but each group maintains its own lines of authority and accountability. This relationship model may be used at the early stages of church planting. As the church grows, the distinctiveness of the two groups becomes a point of stress. The two must acknowledge one another and work together because they are both in the Body of Christ, and the relationship will eventually have to change in order to alleviate tensions and more effectively fulfill the mandate of Christ.

"Modified dichotomy" describes the relationship style that is somewhere between the two extremes. Adopted by many evangelical mission organizations, this is a relationship style where two families live in separate houses in the same village, but they work in the same field. Hence, the church and mission agency share common work responsibilities, but each maintains its distinctive qualities as the local cultural expression of the Body of Christ. Different terms are used to describe this relationship: partnership, association, fellowship, *épauler* or shouldering, and integration. The position of the relationship on the continuum depends on the degree to which the two entities lean toward fusion on the left or dichotomy on the right.

Conclusion: Demonstrate the Oneness of Christ

The form of organization and the picture of the relationship are not as important as the fact that the foreign worker and the local church are able to freely fulfill their respective biblical callings with dignity. Thus, it is imperative that both find that relationship model or picture that frees them to express the cultural image of the church. This biblical image takes into account cultural, political, and social expectations and requirements, so that demonstrating Jesus is foremost. The relationship of a sent-one to the emerging church will determine whether people see Christ in their church, or they see the foreigner in their church. The unity that the world sees in the church will be affected by whether or not the missionary can accept the emerging congregation as the Church, even if this is expressed in a way that is not understandable to him.

Two believers, Makoso and Paul, demonstrated this Christ-like oneness when they served as an itinerant evangelism team. The national church's evangelist, Makoso, was pleased to finally be teamed with a missionary. He had managed the expenses of his ministry without a foreign teammate, using offerings from each campaign. Now that he had a missionary partner, he could have asked for money to increase his income or improve his equipment. Instead, the new partners worked out an agreement whereby offerings continued to pay for all expenses, and mission money was only used for essential purchases that offerings could not cover. Further, they agreed that as the principal evangelist, Makoso would establish his own schedule and be the main preacher. If at any time Paul could attend a meeting, Makoso would step down from preaching for that event. This arrangement allowed the evangelist to be completely independent, while permitting the sent-one to fulfill his principal ministries. Whenever Paul had an unscheduled Sunday, he joined Makoso, sometimes arriving during a worship service. Thanks to their excellent relationship, Makoso would immediately surrender the pulpit to his partner. They both found joy in serving Christ in a relationship that worked well. Makoso's ministry could have become rigid and program oriented. Instead he chose to lead evangelistic campaigns that the local people could afford, and he focused on a working relationship with Paul that harnessed the spiritual gifts of both for the benefit of the kingdom.

In praying for His Bride, Jesus did not ask the Father to take the church out of the world, but to keep her from the evil one (John 17:15). He wanted those in the church to be one just as He and the Father were one. "May they also be in us," He prayed, "so that the world may believe that you have sent me" (John 17:21, NIV). Harmony in the Body of Christ will convince an unbelieving and hostile world that Jesus is the Son sent by the Father. The sent-one must make it his goal to reflect the transcultural oneness in Christ as he and his church partner build relationships that respect the dignity of all. This will free the local followers of Jesus to obey Him, and it will convince outsiders that they need to follow the One who was sent from God.

Chapter 10

The Crisis of Mission Transition

Stay true to your call as a sent-one

THE MOST DIFFICULT period in the history of a national church can be when the mission agency decides to leave the work in the hands of the local believers asking the foreign workers to move on. The process of transition will be easier for all involved if they understand from the beginning that this is part of God's plan, and that each must obey their call. When God leads the sent-one to tell the Story to another people, the church should see it as a reason to rejoice. This is more than passing on the baton. It is obeying the God-given mandate to spread the gospel, for believers have been called to embrace this global vision.

This chapter presents guidelines that facilitate smooth transitioning of foreign workers from the place where they have worked to a new challenge. If we understand the attitude of Scripture regarding our calling, we will be motivated to establish steps for this change.

The Church Chooses the Hard Road

The People's Church of Colombo, Sri Lanka, gave this testimonial:

In 1964, the Foreign Missions Board of the Assemblies of God of USA decided to recall their last missionary from Sri Lanka and to revoke their quota of missionary visas. At the time this seemed to be a fatal blow to the work. Foreign financial support was reduced to $60 a month, just enough to pay for the Chairman's traveling. Some workers resigned. But others, the majority, decided to trust God for their needs. The change-over was difficult, but that was the turning point for the growth of the Assemblies of God in Sri Lanka. It rose to the new challenge. God began to bless the faithful work of His servants. New workers were trained locally. People were added to the church, and the people learned to give. They began to take greater and greater steps of faith. Gradually the work grew in numbers, stability and finance. We look back and realize that it was God who prompted the withdrawal of foreign funds so that the church might grow up and attain its proper stature.[1]

Taking the step of freedom is an important decision, and it may be the most difficult one. The foreign worker and the local church must partner together for the transition to be healthy and ultimately lead both to deeper maturity.

New Testament Perspective on Transition

The parable of the sower teaches us that we need to focus on planting the seed in all soils (Matt. 13:1–9). Jesus' words about the harvest suggest that the most labor-intensive work is that of the planter and cultivator. The harvest will come because people have persevered in the preliminary work (John 4:34–38).

We talk about transition in missions because we believe that there are vast regions where the seed is yet to be planted. Jesus was not satisfied to touch a handful of needy villages. He sent the Seventy "into *every* town where He was about to come" (Luke 10:1, italics added). He further promised that the gospel would be preached "to the *whole* world, ... to *all nations*" before the end would come (Matt. 24:14). Before His ascension, Jesus instructed His followers to "make disciples of *all nations*" (Matt. 28:19) and to go into "*all the world*" (Mark 16:15). Luke's account of this commission describes the ever-widening circles of influence as the Message was told to *all* (Acts 1:8). If we take the words of our Master seriously, we will not be satisfied until there are no people groups remaining who have not heard the Story.

The Apostle Paul was not satisfied to declare the gospel in only one or two cities of Asia Minor. He was ever ready to go to the next town, even if it was sometimes the anger of the crowds that forced him to do so. We are told that during his two-year stay at Ephesus, "all the residents of Asia heard" (Acts 19:10). Paul introduced his global vision to the Roman believers by stating that his ambition was "to preach the gospel, not where Christ has already been named, lest I build on another man's foundation" (Rom. 15:20). The stories about the other apostles going north to Europe, east to India, and south to Africa challenge us. These early believers were so transformed by the resurrection of their Master that they became truly restless. If the people a step further from them had not yet heard the Story, they would go that one step further. Transition was a way of life because the Master had instructed them in that conviction.

Although you may approve of the passion of the apostles, there might be some problems that keep it from happening in your life. I believe at least three true-to-life issues make transition difficult.

First, there are still many peoples who have yet to embrace the Truth. Some might be in your region, where there is an active congregation of Christians, and others might be further away. These distant people often belong to established and organized religions. Their culture is so steeped in the ancient religion that Christianity incites their wrath. This hardness, as we have called it, has caused mission endeavors to prefer more receptive, sometimes animistic, cultures. If a sent-one has had such success with these responsive peoples, to think of working among a resistant people evokes fear. Or if people believe that there will always be unreached people, they might think it useless to endure the stress of relocating to remedy an unsolvable problem.

Second, the church that you have established may still be struggling to survive, and they need your help. You have worked hard to develop their infrastructure and vision and your continued presence could insure that they will become global minded. In addition, there may be other congregations whose self-image is tied to your presence among them, congregations that believe they cannot reflect Christ's image without you. Political or financial restraints might be preventing them from fulfilling the mandate of mission without the organizational base of the Western mission society.

These realities give birth to a third issue that hinders transition. Some workers, who are still successfully involved in the local church, do not want to move on. They have sacrificed their lives to plant and nurture this church and their identity has become enmeshed with the church and its people by whom they are appreciated and admired. Often the mental conflict of transition might cause them to keep adjusting their job description and ministry profile to insure longevity. They will come up with various excuses, which they might think of as "good reasons," to stay behind. But no reason for staying when the Master asks you to go is good enough! Good reasons to stay when the local church needs to walk in dependence on Christ cannot be good. It is best to obey the Master and follow His example. Jesus left the glory of His Father, emptying Himself to take on the form of a servant and man (Phil. 2:6–7). He told the disciples that His leaving would be to their advantage (John 16:5–7). Thus, when Jesus commissioned His disciples, He *sent* them just as the Father had *sent* Him (John 20:21).

Guidelines for Reducing Transition Crisis

The biblical mandate to keep sowing the seed raises a practical but difficult question. How do you transition to new peoples with the blessing of the local church? In response to this crisis, there are certain principles that you will need to bear in mind. The principles shared in this chapter are organized by two major periods in a congregation's maturity. First, I describe guidelines to work with a newly formed assembly, here called the *emerging church*. Then I will describe how transition from an already functioning or *established church*. It must be remembered that every church within the Body of Christ has its own history and character, which will determine the way these principles are applied.

The emerging church

These churches are mostly in the pioneer stage and the congregations are small. Nevertheless we must empower them to become Christ-centered. The six principles mentioned below will help orient the emerging church toward adulthood. If they are applied from the inception of the church, the transition will be less traumatic. These principles should be understood in the context of the Christ-centered church.[2]

A. Clarify your purpose and have an approximate time frame. Share the purpose of your ministry with the local believers. Your strategy should describe the longevity of the mission agency's presence. Even if you may not immediately have a specific transition date in mind, the purpose statement should clarify the maturing nature of the emerging church as an indication of the transition time. Seek the support of the emerging church in helping you reach that goal.

Sometimes assemblies are formed out of a refugee ministry or a development work. The transient nature of refugee life will help you to convey to the believers that you are a temporary presence, but they will be the enduring church. Your purpose is to prepare them to take the assembly back to their homeland so that even when the project comes to an end, the church will not.

B. Train and empower leaders as they emerge. Put in place leadership training models that are culturally manageable, as this will enhance the natural selection of leaders through the Spirit-led processes of the local Body. Teach them to trust the Holy Spirit in their selection and growth, and then turn over the responsibilities to them as if you have already moved on. Challenge the leaders-in-training to participate with you as you seek other unreached people, to help them understand your vision and expand their worldview.

C. Develop a forum for discussion. The local church leaders need to be able to openly discuss the future of their church and your role in it. This will happen more easily if they have been empowered with dignity from the beginning, and when they feel comfortable with you. You must gently remind them that they are fully responsible for the church in their country. Use the discussion format to affirm them in their continuing role as its leaders. The evaluation tool in Appendix B will help them gain a picture of a Christ-centered church that is not in the shadow of the mission agency. This tool must be taught and frequently used to focus their attention on the priorities of such a church.

D. Prioritize ministry opportunities that enhance spontaneous growth. Help the local believers develop spiritual ministries that they can lead. These should to grow out of their felt needs, not from your perception of a need. Be careful not to infuse outside money to enhance programs that the locals will not be able to continue. A ministry will enhance church growth if it continues to function even when the foreign worker is absent.

E. Move on! You need to release the believers so that they learn to depend on the Holy Spirit. This will allow Him to lead and mature those whom He has called, and it will allow God to bring the increase. Don't wait until the people have reached a level of maturity where they "doing church" and "doing theology" in ways that you approve. Instead, aim to equip the saints (Eph. 4:12) so that they will stand firm after you have left. Waiting to do this when you retire may impede the church's maturity. The transition should be a joyful expression of the church's confidence that the Holy Spirit will not permit what He has birthed to die.

F. Keep in touch with the Church. Post-transition communication needs to become a habit, for it is at this point that the church-mission relationship becomes that of two churches, rather than that of church and sending agency. Contact can be maintained through national organizations, through an international fellowship of emerging churches planted by the same agency, and other such groups. The mission team can, at the invitation of the church, conduct special training courses or send guest speakers for church retreats and pastors' training conferences. Likewise, the emerging church can send members to participate in the church planting team's ministry in a new region.

The established church

This type of church is one that has existed for a number of years in a place where the mission presence has been prolonged. The people have attained a level of maturity, with the leaders taking hold of their ministries. This description would also apply to indigenously established churches that were founded by local believers in an area without the presence of a foreign mission. In this latter case, if a foreign mission wants to start a partnership with the indigenous church, it will do well to follow the guidelines given below, as these can help build productive relationships.

Foreign workers must work with the national church to reach the goal of complete autonomy, always keeping in focus the cultural factors relating to adulthood. I propose eight steps to take in the process toward transition, understanding that this is painful in contexts where years of cooperation have generated fond memories and a strong emotional bond. It is human nature to cling to such comforts and avoid the crisis transition.

A. Select a mutually acceptable forum in which all parties can freely exchange ideas. This can consist of members of the church's executive committee and selected members of the mission team, but there must be more church representation. A church leader, such as the senior pastor or general secretary, should preside at the sessions. The agenda, completed in advance, should focus more on plans and joint projects than on problem-solving and financial issues. Care should be exercised that these meetings not become negotiation sessions in which the local church is asking the mission agency for money. Costs for the joint meetings should be equally shared, if not totally financed by the church. Written minutes, reflecting joint decisions and responsibilities, should be published for all interested personnel within a month of the conclusion of each session. All participating local churches should be informed of decisions by their leadership, not by the missionary or his mission agency.

B. Clarify the mission statement of each group involved in the transition. This needs to be done on a regular basis so that rumor and misunderstanding do not start fires that leaders constantly need to quench. The mission statements of each group should be frequently publicized in a form that local pastors can present to their congregations.

To fulfill the long-term implications of the transition, both mission and church leaders must evaluate all ministries against their respective purpose statements. They may discover an organizational structure or an institution that the national church will not be able to financially support on its own. In some cases, local leaders may have to completely revamp the structure of an organization in order to make it more manageable for them.[3] This will also keep the ministry in a more contextual format. If ministries exist that the locals cannot manage, a decision must be mutually made to bring that program to a close. Closing a program or handing it over to the church may require withdrawing the foreign worker who operated it. Therefore, missionaries must always keep in mind that ministries belong to the local church. After the church has tried to manage a program without success, its leaders must be permitted the dignity of deciding to end it.

C. Train all church leaders and missionaries in biblical eccle-siology and relevant missiological issues. The over-riding goal of this training should be to teach all participants—local believers, their leaders, and foreign workers—on the same biblical value system and its implications for growth. Plan forums to train church leaders in subjects related to the church, including God's mission for the church, church-mission polity, and other relevant subjects. These should enable local leaders to take corrective measures in ministries that are not contributing to growth. The church's leadership training institutes should also include courses in church growth and the missiology of global mission events. These must openly teach and evaluate the struggles of the Christ-centered church and the effects of foreign involvement. The concept of the missionary as a sent-one who establishes assemblies among other people groups must become the standard vocabulary of all concerned.

D. Increase church participation in the ministries while decreasing missionary involvement. All programs must aim to train and empower native leaders. As new leaders emerge, encourage them to become involved in ministries for which they are gifted and to function in a manner that is both biblical and culturally appro-priate. Challenge the church to partner with the mission in seeking unreached people. This will help them understand the vision of the mission. It will also expand their worldview and keep everyone's focus on Christ's mandate to reach the unreached.

In all shared ministries or programs we must aim for the church to become financially self-reliant. Reductions in financial aid by the mission are more effective when not mandated by the mission, but understood and mutually accepted. Encourage and train local leaders in financial accountability with a view to deepening their dependence on God.

E. Transition missionaries according to a known plan.[4] Unplea-sant surprises create tensions in the mission-church relationship. To avoid this, the plans for the transition to self-reliance must be known and understood by everyone. All workers must be aware that the church belongs to the local people and should therefore be operated by them. Use natural circumstances to move foreign workers out of church-related ministries and local leaders into the work. For example, when a sent-one retires or returns home on furlough, or if he is forced to evacuate due to political turmoil or illness, don't replace him with another foreign worker.

F. Permit the church to be the Church in its own culture. Missionaries need to allow the local church to function as the Body of Christ should in this culture. Local believers should be encouraged to choose indigenous ways of worship and giving, witness and mission, teaching and training, and leading and serving. This principle presupposes that the foreign worker sought to plant the church in the host culture without making it an image of his home church in a foreign country. Appropriate contextualization is necessary from the start, because the missionary is accountable to God through his sending church and the local leaders are accountable to God through their emerging church. Both churches serve the same God, but the cultural contexts in which they do so might be radically different.

The concept of the "foreign expert" or "church facilitator" to describe the sent-one has emerged in the late twentieth century. Some missionaries have used this definition to strengthen their argument to stay in a situation instead of moving on not realizing that the long-term "facilitator" will create an unhealthy, co-dependent relationship with the local church. As true sent-ones, we must allow ourselves to move on in the manner of the Apostle Paul. Tension will be reduced, even avoided, when we remember that we are sent, and facilitate just long enough to open doors to go to others who have not heard the Story.

G. Move joyfully to the new challenge. Each culture has its way of expressing goodbyes, and we must allow local assemblies to do it in their way. Let the people demonstrate their thanksgiving and joy as they send you off, perhaps even with some of their own workers.

H. Keep in touch. As discussed in the previous section, we must be committed to regular communication. Not only must we stay in touch with the local assembly, but we must also connect them with other groups. Foreign workers err when they remain the sole channel between the planted churches and other groups. Although helpful, this may cause the local church to see itself as dependent on the missionary for its adult identity. An effective transition encourages the emerging church to see itself as Christ's Body and not the property of the mission agency. Hence, the mission agency and its missionary must graciously step out of the picture.

Conclusion

Transition is essential for the local body to establish its identity as a Christ-centered church. How it is organized at birth will not change its essence but it may affect the church's reaching maturity. What we need to do is allow the emerging church to make decisions without our continued presence or involvement, so that our moving on will not be a traumatic event for them.

Some sent-ones might have found this chapter difficult to understand or accept, especially if they view transition as a threat to their personhood. Alan Tippett had stinging words for those who have difficulty letting a church fully transition to local leadership.

The sending Church has to send missionaries or fraternal workers who are culturally ready for self-emptying of their ... [home culture], for the "drama" of church-planting and of church growth has to be "played" in "acts" and "scenes" radically different from the dramas of the last hundred years.... The door is no longer open for the ethnocentric or foreign missionary. Although every situation is unique, the one common feature, the "given" of every situation, is that the Church in its planting or its growing should be a "thing of the soil." This means the indigenizing of the missionary must be a major feature of his training. The genuineness of his kenosis should be his humble and continuous prayer.[5]

In the passage above, Tippett employs the Greek word *kenosis*, which Paul used to describe the self-emptying of Christ (Phil. 2:7), when speaking of the process of allowing a local assembly to become mature and authentically indigenous. A lifestyle of self-emptying will be required of the missionary, to allow the national church to become all that God intends it to be.

Chapter 11

The Crisis of Money and Mission

The Christ-centered church depends primarily on Jesus

THE APOSTLE PAUL'S warning regarding money applies equally to the foreign worker and the national church: "For the love of money is a root of all sorts of evil, and some by longing for it have wandered away from the faith, and pierced themselves with many a pang. But flee from these things, you man of God: and pursue righteousness, godliness, faith, love, perseverance and gentleness" (1 Tim. 6:10–11). Many emerging Christian assemblies have lost their spiritual vitality as a result of financial struggles. Congregations planted in developing nations by Western missionaries often find themselves unable to function according to the biblical mandate because they are not financially independent. Their attitude about money hinders them from depending on Christ's sufficiency and is the source of untold crises.

Depend on God

Knowing the principles of financial dependence on God is good, but it is not as effective as learning by experience. Examples throughout church history encourage us to believe that total reliance on God is not just possible but necessary. The following stories from churches in Asia and Africa remind us that followers of Christ deeply desire financial freedom.

The Lisu church of China

The Lisu are a tribal group living in the mountains near Burma, Vietnam, and China. Looked down upon by ethnic Chinese, the Lisu were extremely poor when James Fraser, a missionary with the

China Inland Mission (CIM), began taking the gospel to them in the 1920s. Fraser could have easily solicited funding in the CIM fashion to help these people mature in Christ more quickly. Instead, he chose to share their poverty, convinced that a self-propagating church needed to be self-supporting. He believed that if the church were to accept foreign funding, it would be weak, and he therefore encouraged evangelists and other church ministers to serve God without pay. As a result, evangelists went wherever the Holy Spirit led them, learning to trust Him to provide for their needs. Believers built meeting places from their limited resources. Students attended the monthly Bible training schools supported by their family and church. A pioneer in applying the concept of financial freedom, Fraser explained his conviction thus:

> There was a time when I should have been [reluctant] of pressing the subject [of receiving outside funding] any further, with people living in such poverty. But I know the Lisu better now, and so proceed to give them a good round of reproof for suggesting such a meager contribution. They did not much like it, naturally enough, and some of them grumbled and argued against me vigorously.... I pointed out that they were proposing to give to the work of the Lord, who had given His life for them, just about one-sixteenth part of the money they usually spent on tobacco and betel nut ...[1]

When the Maoist revolution reached their region, the Lisu were better prepared to face its onslaught than other Christian groups, for they were already reliant upon God.

A South African church

Several years ago, the pastor of a church in Cape Town, South Africa, was invited to speak in churches in the United States. During his visit he was presented with many offers of financial assistance, but the pastor had this testimony:

> One Sunday evening after preaching in a local church, I was given the offering in cash. They did not write a check for the amount, but simply gave it to me as it was. As I counted the money, I came across an American five-cent piece with a buffalo on it—a buffalo nickel.

When I saw this, I immediately associated it with the message of my sister-in-law's dream. I knew that God was telling me that while in America I was not to pursue money....

The next morning ... a wealthy businessman offered to write a check for any amount. Remembering God's instructions, I replied, "Thank you very much, but the Lord takes care of me and my people in His own way." He gave me no money.

[On] the plane ... to Johannesburg a wealthy white South African businessman ... offered to help me financially ... I told him, "Thank you very much, but the Lord takes care of me and my people in His own way." I got no money from that man either.

I returned home to discover that the people of my local congregation wanted to build their own church building. We have since built a new sanctuary completely from the funds of our own people, and we did not need any "buffalos" from overseas.[2]

Stories like this are being repeated around the world, as local assemblies are obeying God by depending on Him to provide. This decision is often a difficult one, but the joy and self-esteem it generates far outweigh any frustration experienced in the process.

Dependence on Christ

The Bible is clear in its teaching concerning money and its management by believers and unbelievers. Jesus must have shocked His listeners when He told them, "Where your treasure is, there will your heart be also" (Matt. 6:21). A person's habit of giving directly affects his worship, his dignity, his sense of well-being, and his walk with God. Five biblical principles of giving will help the believer focus on Christ.

1. Giving to God is humanity's response of worship

A divine intuition to worship has placed within the human soul the desire to respond to the creator. Throughout history, people have responded to God (or the gods) by giving gifts and sacrifices. Humankind was created in the image of God (Gen. 1:26) and as such, stands in dignity before its creator. The eyes of this created humanity see that "the heavens are telling the glory of God; and their expanse is declaring the work of His hands" (Ps. 19:1). Every culture has an innate understanding of the existence of a Higher Being "because that which is known about God is evident within them; for God made it evident to them" (Rom. 1:19–20). Those who respond in worship join the creation in telling the glory of God.

This response of thanksgiving is recorded from the early chapters of the Bible. The first two sons of Adam and Eve responded to God through giving: Cain worshiped by giving offerings from his garden and Abel sacrificed from his flock (Gen. 4:3–4). When Noah emerged from the ark, he responded the Lord in reverence and praise by offering burnt offerings that were like a pleasing aroma (Gen. 8:20). Abraham distinguished himself as a man of worship for in every encounter with God, he offered a sacrifice on the altar. His greatest sacrifice was that of his son, Isaac, whom Jehovah would replace with a ram (Gen. 22). When Abraham encountered the high priest, Melchizedek, his worship-response was to give one tenth or a tithe of all the spoils (Gen. 14:20; Heb. 7:4).

Abraham and his descendants knew that all they owned came from Jehovah. Worship without giving was not an option in Israel. Moses taught the Israelites that no one attending the Feast of Unleavened Bread should appear before the Lord empty-handed (Ex. 23:15), and King David challenged them to give offerings for the temple (1 Chron. 29:14–16). The New Testament believers also worshiped God with their gifts as they were taught (see for example 1 Cor. 16:1–2). Paul carried the offerings collected in Asia Minor to help the Jerusalem church (1 Cor. 16:3–4; 2 Cor. 8:1).

If worship in giving is a response springing out of the image of God, then withholding gifts dishonors that image. New believers should be encouraged from the day they turn to Christ to see giving as worship and that it need not be limited to coins or paper bills. Giving is an act of sharing all that God has provided and the worship leaders should encourage giving of any kind of possession, be it produce, time, clothes, or money.

Giving is the responsibility of every believer

The people of Israel were taught by Moses to give freely and joyfully. In preparing to construct the Tabernacle, leaders encouraged every family to give to Jehovah, and *everyone* whose heart stirred him came joyfully and gave freely of his possessions (Ex.

35:5, 21, 29). In the end, Moses had to order the giving to stop because the amount received was "much more than enough" (Ex. 36:7). During the reign of Solomon, the construction of the house of prayer fell on the Israelites who, with their king, paid for everything, even the material given by the king of Lebanon. They had learned that all things come from the Lord (1 Chron. 29:14) and that each one must use that wealth to worship and serve Him.

The New Testament teaches that believers gave at least a tenth of their income (Matt. 23:23), and that they do so willingly and sacrificially. The idea is to give from the heart, as in the account of the poor woman who gave, not just her tithe, but everything she had (Luke 21:1-4).

2. Attitudes of giving are more important than the value of the items given

Moses taught the children of Israel to give joyfully and "with a willing heart" (Ex. 35:5, 21, 29). All sections of Jewish society, rich and poor, responded together in worship and a total consecration to God (Deut. 26).

Jesus taught that giving is to be done in secret without worrying about who sees, because the Father in heaven is watching (Matt. 6:3–4). In Luke 21, Jesus commended the woman who gave two cents for the value of her sacrifice that was greater than the quantity given by others. The Apostle Paul later taught that true gratitude is marked by generosity that exceeds the tithe (Rom. 12:8; 1 Tim. 6:18), and that giving that is purposeful and cheerful glorifies God (2 Cor. 9:7, 13). God is the provider, and happy are those who learn to be content in every circumstance (Phil. 4:12, 19).

Giving reveals the spiritual character of the believers, who give cheerfully, liberally, willingly, and without constraint. This implies that church leaders should avoid imposing a giving structure or system, such as tithe cards attached to baptism certificates, fees for baptism, seat rentals, and the like.

4. All believers are to be faithful stewards

The wisest man that ever lived encouraged people to be just in their financial dealings because God hates dishonesty (Pro. 11:1;

16:11; 20:10). God had long held the leaders of Israel accountable to correctly use the wealth that came from worshipers, and Moses taught the priests to "do no wrong in judgment, in measurement of weight, or capacity" (Lev. 19:35–36). They were warned that their offerings that they must have "a full and just weight" so that their life would be prolonged (Deut. 25:15). When the priests came to the Temple, their gift needed to be the best, and a priest had to take care of the offering as if it were the most precious possession. In the Old Testament, Moses (Num. 16:15), Joseph (Gen. 39:6), and Daniel (Dan. 6:5) are presented as examples of integrity in wealth management. Moses was a steward of God's wealth, while others were stewards of pagan riches. During the reign of Jehoash, the temple was rebuilt and refurbished with integrity because the king required that Jehoiada, the priest, give account for the gifts and the workers (2 Ki. 12:6–16). Later, during the exilic period, Nehemiah appointed "reliable men" to care for the storehouse of Jerusalem (Neh. 13:13).

Bad financial stewardship brought judgment (Num. 18: 32). For instance, severe punishment fell on the sons of Eli who took portions of the offerings that were not theirs (1 Sam. 2:12–17; 4:11). The Old Testament comes to a close with the prophet Malachi's word of judgment on the priests whose dishonest management and greed had sadly stopped God's blessing to His people (Mal. 1–3).

Accountability for God's money was expected in the New Testament as well. Jesus repeatedly taught that a steward of the Lord must be faithful (Matt. 25:14–30; Luke 12:42; 16:1–13), and the Apostle Paul himself practiced careful money management. When sending the gift from the Gentile converts to the Jerusalem church, he sent letters attesting to the generosity of the givers. He was willing to do everything he could to ensure that the gifts were the correctly accounted for the gifts (1 Cor. 16:2-4; 2 Cor. 8:18–21).

5. Personal poverty or wealth do *not* change the Christian's responsibility to give

Moses did not ask that the rich give more or the poor less, but he instructed everyone "of a willing heart" to give (Ex. 35:5). The tithe was applied to all classes of Israel (Deut. 14, 26), and Jesus and the apostles did not exclude certain people from giving. Paul used the example of the Philippian church to teach that poverty need not hinder generosity (2 Cor. 8:2), which is contrary to what many Christians say today. Believers were commended for giving despite their poverty, according to their ability and of their own accord, in the same way that they had given themselves to the Lord (2 Cor. 8:3). Paul cited the Old Testament principle that the one who sows sparingly will reap sparingly (2 Cor. 9:6, 8–11), a principle that excludes none. He used the Philippian assembly as an example to encourage the Corinthian church to give generously, and he commended the Philippian church for their gift to the "mother church" in Jerusalem, which did not exempt that congregation from future sharing.

The Hindering Foreigner

Financial freedom and dependence are not the result of spontaneous generation—they do not spring to life overnight. They are the product of cultural and social values. Attitudes drive money. A sent-one's goal is to establish a congregation whose members depend fully on God for their material needs, he will make decisions and introduce procedures that encourage reliance on God. On the other hand, if he doesn't consciously practice self-reliance in his life, the local believers will tend not to do so either.

Certain wrong beliefs and unhealthy relational patterns between local congregations and the sent-one create a financial bondage to the mission. I will present four of the most common hindrances to self-reliance, which keep local believers focused on their need for the foreigner rather than pursuing their greater need for God.

1. The mission is the great financial resource

The foreigner is seen as having an endless supply of wealth that must be shared with the poor members of God's family. This belief arises from the fact that the mission agency or missionary is usually able to provide financial assistance for evangelistic campaigns, missionary outreaches, and buildings for schools, churches, hospitals, or clinic. The channel of outside resources is so consistent that local believers may refer to the donor as God's provision. Even if the mission agency experiences a financial crisis, the level of subsidy to the national church does not drop. Funding to the mission team operations and missionary salaries might be reduced but in the eyes of the local people, the money flow is the same. Furthermore, the mission's financial cutbacks are not taken seriously by local believers who think that cutbacks are a normal part of life, since they don't have much to begin with.

2. Missionary assignments are a financial asset to the local church

The missionary is seen primarily as a channel for financial aid and his spiritual or evangelistic contribution is sometimes viewed as secondary. Hence church leaders, almost without exception, prefer a missionary to be appointed to their congregation rather than to an unreached people group. This may explain why, when a worker is sent to an unreached people, some ask, "Why do you keep sending missionaries where there is no church?"

3. Partnership is sometimes one-sided

The national church perceives the church-mission relationship as one in which the mission gives the money and they do the work. You may have heard the slogan, "The mission helps us be like the Church!" As a result, negotiations between the church and the mission organization may become just that—negotiation! Many national church leaders do not consider partnership agreements as valid if the mission cannot give finances, and partnerships sometimes break down over financial issues.

4. The foreign worker's lifestyle looks like it is always improving

The sent-one is seen to have the money to get new cars, even when he shares about the miraculous way in which God gave it to him. The locals believe that for some missionaries God provides a new car every term, and for others He provides *two* cars! And they wonder why God does not provide for them like that. The missionary appears to have the means to maintain his higher standard of living. He receives crates and barrels to set up house, he does not have to work his field, and he can afford to have servants and give loans. The mission organization is also seen as rich. It can purchase properties for new stations and rent a missionary residence, which some cultures consider to be money down the drain.

Strategic Consequences of Dependency

Kingdom growth is affected when the sending agency, the foreign worker, and the planted church continue habits of financial dependence that are very difficult to overcome. The following are ten strategic consequences of this dependency.

1. Evangelism and church planting by the national church are hindered, especially expansion into new areas and to unreached people groups. The church leaders might protest that they don't have the financial means to send and support their evangelist, and they will be correct if the missionary helped them set up a mission committee patterned on the Western model. Research reveals that individual and lifestyle witness that is culturally appropriate is more successful than helping the national church support its foreign mission structure.

2. Worship and meeting centers are built with difficulty, because the hosts think that they cannot raise the funds. As the church expands, constructing worship centers is seen as the duty of the foreigner. This is especially true where the foreigner contributes more towards building expenses and has done most of the construction work, leaving little decision making to the local leadership. The mission might have sent a short-term construction team to "do the work right," or the sent-one might have supervised the work of local builders. These situations can lead to problems of financial mismanagemen, and reduce the believers' spiritual motivation. If building the meeting place is not in their own hands, then the responsibility to see it filled with people may not be seen as theirs either.

3. Planting city churches is hindered. The local believers claim that they need the crowd with its financial resources in a central meeting place. This reveals a flawed evangelism strategy and vision. They also think that they cannot afford to pay a city pastor until the new group is mature. This misconception is related to a lack of obedience to the Great Commission and trust in God's provision. As a result, the church will not take the risk to hive off a new congregation.

4. Personal dignity of the national church is undermined. The locals often say things like, "We can't own what we don't pay for." Or, "We must make decisions on the basis of how that affects the

continuing flow of money." Or, "We don't hold the destiny of our own church because we can't support ourselves." These beliefs arise from a faulty self-perception. Continuing dependency feels like a form of slavery to the father mission or the foreign worker, and it ultimately ends up becoming a self-fulfilling prophecy.

5. Spiritual obedience of the church is stifled. Church members hesitate to give adequate offerings because they know that the mission will come to the rescue, and their local leaders cannot motivate giving because the need is covered by a security blanket of foreign funds. Church members are unable to pressure leaders to be honest in managing church money because, should they apply pressure by withholding financial support, the leader would still survive by receiving foreign aid. Furthermore, leaders may be hindered from creatively tackling their own financial misman-agement because the money used is not from local resources.

6. A love-hate relationship with the mission develops, as the locals love the aid but resent the missionary for not allowing them to do what they know that they should do. Anger will rise toward the mission or sent-one that reduces or ends support. Or jealousy will flare up when another church receives more aid. Roots of bitterness will spring up if the mission agency does not give what is perceived to be able to give.[3]

7. The accusation of Neo-colonialism is leveled against the mis-sion agency because the financial gift introduces the external obligation of accountability and stipulations (also called "guide-lines") for use of the grant. Whether true or false, this accusation increases tensions between the missionary and the church. However, this is not to say that the donor should not insist on accountability. It can also be used to manipulate the missionary to give more money! In this case, Neo-colonialism is an accurate critique of what has happened, because the donors thought that the gift needed to be given under stipulation. In many relation-based cultures, giving something with an associated condition for its use implies that the recipient is unable to exercise discipline or good sense. Hence, the recipient cannot maintain his dignity or integrity and also accept the gift.

8. Manipulation for equal distribution of wealth is a tool by which a group of churches may pressure the mission to give more money. Sometimes, if church X received help, churches Y and Z also demand to be treated with fairness, which results in a type of blackmail between churches and mission leaders.

9. Both partners violate shared responsibility. As a church-mission relationship model, partnership implies that there be at least 50/50 participation in certain ministries for a time. When one side has the donor's role and the dignity of the other feels violated, the relationship is no longer a partnership but closer to a "paternalship."

10. Tensions mount over control of the money and church decisions. The temptation to influence by money can be great. The donor must avoid the attitude that would say, "I gave this money, therefore I should have a say in how it is used." In some cases, the financial gift may cause the local church to feel obligated to deal with an internal problem in the missionary's way rather than use an approach that is culturally more effective. For example, a sent-one's home church underwrites most of the cost for a locally trained church planting team that will go to an unreached people group. The missionary who transmits the funds to the national church suggests some local evangelists for the new team. Then the church leaders propose their names for the team, but feel obliged to accept the donor's selection. Over the years, the foreign-supported team demands more aid and becomes less effective. Tension mounts when the missionary accuses the church leaders of mismanaging their unproductive evangelists. The church leaders try to correct the crisis only to be blocked when the local evangelists say they owe allegiance first to the donors.

God's sent-ones and the local church need to somehow break this vicious cycle of unhealthy attitudes. The enduring growth of an emerging church depends on a Christ-ward focus, even in money. Jesus clearly taught, "No one can serve two masters; for either he will hate the one and love the other, or he will be devoted to the one and despise the other. You cannot serve God and mammon" (Matt. 6:24). The foreign worker can teach dependence on Christ through his lifestyle and his financial dealings with the people he disciples.

A More Dignified Way: Rely on Christ

Do you find yourself in a financially binding relationship with those whom you call brothers and sisters in Christ? This can develop even if you are seeking the same goal as the emerging church—to fully trust in God rather than relying on outside resources.

A healthy church will, from its inception, teach through word and deed that the believer depends on God alone. This kind of financial Christ-centered focus may take on a different appearance with each culture. Therefore, the biblical concept of the God-reliant church must be studied and developed in the local context.

Where the emerging church has become dependent on the mission, the process of transitioning out of foreign support can cause tension and misunderstandings. This occurs because money involves people and their personhood, but some of the tensions can be reduced if the steps toward reliance on Christ are planned with local believers. Leaders of the mission and the church must work together to correct people's perceptions about their responsibility to God in areas of financial management.

Transition to reliance on God is based on one primary presupposition: that full adherence (legal, emotional, psychological, and spiritual) to a faith movement will result when the people of that movement take full responsibility for its survival. Before the following steps can take effect, spiritual revival must move through the denomination or groups of churches.[4] Freedom from the vice of dependency requires resolve and determination that only the Spirit of God can implant in the local leaders and their congregations. Beyond the work of the Holy Spirit, there are eight important steps that we can incorporate into mission-church procedures that will lead to freedom.

1. Mission leaders and administrators need to be convinced that the church must be Christ-reliant

Coming to this decision may require them to carefully research all areas of their organization's ministry. If necessary, they must consult missiologists who can give a biblical and cultural perspective on the issues. Once mission leaders and sent-ones are committed to the concept, the national leaders must reach the same conviction so that everyone in authority is pursuing the same biblical goals for the church.

2. Train foreign workers about financial Christ-reliance

All foreign workers must accept the concept of financial freedom in Christ. Through prayer and Bible study, we can lead our mission team to understand biblical principles about their relationship with the emerging church. We must study and evaluate personal financial lifestyles and how the different applications of the principle affect the gospel in the host culture. All members of the mission team must agree to establish a biblical philosophy for money management in relationships with church and local believers.

3. Train national church leaders who will train the local believers in financial Christ-reliance

A curriculum on financial obedience must be included in seminaries and other pastoral training institutions. Conduct prayer and Bible study retreats aimed at spiritual renewal and challenge people to obey the biblical guidelines related to financial freedom. Lead them to take responsibility for their church, using positive terminology such as "reach financial freedom" and "developing dignity." Trust the Holy Spirit to implant a vision of the financial freedom that they can transfer to the believers. Review together biblical ecclesiology as it relates to the Christ-centered church and its relationship to the missionaries, and help the emerging church to understand the biblical meaning of "missionary" as it applies to their context. Teach them biblical principles of giving, tithing, and management of offerings and other sources of wealth. All of this must be contextualized to their local setting, and it must help the people to visualize their own desires for financial integrity, dignity, and freedom. This goal is not quickly attained. We must give people time to work through the information and to complete their training process so that the vision is understood at all levels of the church. In addition, we must enable them to understand how this training and the established goals will lead them to fulfill their spiritual responsibility to God and to one another with integrity.

4. Church leaders must take full responsibility for implementing this principle

In conjunction with the above teaching, church leaders need to discuss and plan the complex steps to leading a ministry in which the foreigner no longer has influence. This may require the assistance of an outside group or resource that will help the leaders to understand and clarify their desire. For example, Glenn Schwartz of World Mission Associates has seen positive change as a consultant who meets with local African leaders, motivating them to take responsibility for their ministries.

Many of the older mission agencies have long since turned the work over to the local church, but often their presence is still very real. Tension may develop when the church's vision calls for restructuring the programs or closing an institution or a costly ministry. In this case, the missionaries must be prepared to submit their agenda to that of the church.

5. Clearly communicate financial agreements to the church members and sent-ones

The questions and differing opinions concerning the direction toward a church's financial Christ-reliance will be heatedly discussed among believers. If the mission and church are cooperating, many of these goals and procedures will be determined together. The following guidelines will lead to freedom.

A. Remove all financial subjects from church-mission negotiations. These should be handled on a church-mission joint committee and passed on to the mission board, as outlined by a policy that would need to be established. However, ending financial negotiations needs to be a long-term and mutually valued goal and there should be no palavering on these subjects after a point.

B. Set a financial participation principle that everyone understands. If the mission considers itself in a partnership with the church, then it would seem appropriate to begin with at least a fifty-fifty financial principle. Beyond that, there must be a progressive reduction scale for decreasing subsidy down to the level of financial freedom that the partners have selected. The agreement reached on this principle must be clarified, to avoid manipulation of funds or personnel. For example, the church and mission team may decide to share costs in all projects, even emergencies. When the local church has raised their portion, the mission will provide theirs.

The donor agency or missionary must not provide any financial support for the national church's administrative structure or personnel. The Christ-dependent church must have Christ-reliant leaders, and local churches will often not adequately support their administrator in the future if they are not doing so now. Furthermore, receiving financial aid for administration may breed dishonesty in money management, which churches find hard to rectify.

C. Agree to a unilateral donor reduction principle. Establish the understanding that when the mission is obligated to cut its budget, this cut will affect subsidies to the church at the same percentage that it affects the mission. The mission would need to continue reductions even if the church does not provide the equivalent or determined increase in participation. However, if church leaders decide to advance to 100% God-reliance instead of using a progressive scale, this must be honored. It is biblically and missiologically correct that relying on Christ would enable the national church to support its functioning institutions at 100%.

D. Rescind all further increases in grants and subsidies. Set a donation ceiling in local currency and choose an internal limit on funding for special projects. This includes formulating a procedure for giving grants according to policies set by they joint committee or field leadership committees, but take care that these policies do not lead to dependency in a different way.

6. Develop a mutually understood plan for the deployment (transition) of foreign workers

This plan must conform to the mandate and mission statement of the agency and also encourage local church goals for relying on God. It may mean that after a certain a period, the foreigners will be withdrawn. This could potentially create misunderstandings if explanations are made using the wrong words. The mission must therefore spend enough time explaining the new deployment to church leadership. Sometimes local leaders may realize that the mission or missionary are a hindrance to the local church and may ask them to leave. In such cases, the foreigner must leave graciously, grateful that the national church is maturing in Christ. Remaining could cause the church to be disobedient to God.

If the maturing process requires the local church and the mission to pursue financial readjustments, each one must remember that they are *people* working with *people* to bring the kingdom of God to all *peoples*. Institutions are composed of *people*, therefore *people must understand* God's plan for them.

Conclusion

Arriving at dependence on God is difficult if the existing church has become accustomed to the mission dole. However, if God's people realize that full reliance on Him for financial needs is the best way, they will be open to receiving courage from the Holy Spirit. This may be harder for those who have served under the mission presence for many years, and they may feel nostalgic for the good old days. But fond memories need not hinder anyone from taking steps that will release the church from financial bondage and fully unleash the believers to seek first God's kingdom and His righteousness (Matt 6:33). The benefit of doing so, Jesus promises, is that everything else will fall into place.

Chapter 12

The Crisis of Being vs. Doing

*Find joy that your name is written in the
Book of Life*

WHY DO SOME missionaries want to change the Message? Would finding a newer, better method make the gospel more acceptable? But is the core of the cross-cultural crisis to improve the good news or to share it more effectively? What is your motive for wanting to change your method of doing mission?

Most societies have a value system that determines a person's importance by his or her contribution to the survival of the family. The person who cannot help ensure survival is considered a burden and, therefore, cannot be maintained. In some societies a baby born with mental retardation or a physical handicap is thrown to the animals. While we might be horrified at the thought, don't we also place a high value on performance?

Let's imagine a scenario. You felt called to cross-cultural mission service and joined a training institute to be equipped. You left your parents and your country hoping to integrate into a different world, but you suddenly found yourself in the ever-tightening grip of something known as *expectations*. On the one hand, you worried about what the local people might say about you ("Will they think I'm strange?"), and at the same time, you were concerned about the opinion of the mission board ("Will the mission director think I'm productive?"). To add to these concerns, you wanted to be popular with your colleagues ("What if they don't like me?"). The tension between these three conflicting values finally became greater than you could bear, making you discouraged enough to consider throwing in the towel.

You recognize the scene, and you've heard some of the common reactions to the resulting stress:

"Why don't these people just get it?"

"I want to stay, but I need my support group."

"I'm tired of producing statistics!"

"Let's leave these people to their destiny!"

"At least the people back home care."

The purpose of this chapter is to look at your idea of success and to help you develop goals that you can meet. This will enable you to transcend the stress arising from burdensome expectations imposed by others, including the local culture, the mission agency, and your ministry colleagues.

The Example of Hudson Taylor[1]

Hudson Taylor (1832-1905) obeyed the Holy Spirit's calling and prepared himself for missionary service in China. Arriving in 1853, he followed the policy of his missionary society and learned the local Chinese dialect, and he later obeyed the Spirit's prompting to remove those physical and cultural trappings that hindered the Chinese from hearing his Message. For example, he began to dress like the Chinese men. This caused tension with his missionary colleagues, but it made him more acceptable to the local people.

As the tension mounted, Taylor followed the Spirit's direction by separating from the Chinese Evangelization Society and forming the China Inland Mission (CIM). He recruited missionaries for this first "faith mission." Each sent-one depended entirely on God to provide the financial and prayer backing. Taylor became the leader of a team whose missionaries were from England's working classes, and together they went to the remotest regions of China.

The workers encountered constant opposition to the gospel. The locals hated the "foreign devils" and some even accused them of stealing Chinese children. Social unrest sometimes led to the death of missionaries. Taylor and his family faced repeated illness and his wife would eventually succumb to fatigue from overwork. They buried two children in China and had to send the older ones back to England for education, enduring a separation of six years.

Hudson Taylor continued to serve faithfully despite these hardships, but in his soul he felt overwhelmed by a sense of inadequacy. In 1869 he wrote to his mother: "My responsibilities increase, and I am consequently always in need of special grace to complete the task.... Often I am tempted to believe that a man as full of sin as I am cannot be a child of God...."[2]

During this period of self-doubt, a letter from his colleague, Mr. McCarthy, opened his eyes to the source of his struggle.

> This is my deep conviction today.... We must not pursue great personal efforts and support grand battles on our own, but *abide* in Christ, look to Him, trust in Him to vanquish our corrupt nature, rest in the love of the all powerful Savior, in the conscious joy of *complete* salvation, of the deliverance from *all sin* (it is His Word); want His will to be sovereign in us.... That Christ might be literally our *all*, this seems to me to be the only secret of power, the only foundation of unshakable joy. May He help us to experience His fathomless fullness.[3]

Taylor would tell his colleagues at Chiankiang that, upon reading McCarthy's letter, "the light shined in my soul. I saw Jesus and when I saw Him, Oh! What joy filled me!" He wrote a joyful letter to his sister, Amelia Broomhall, on October 17, 1869, telling her that the Holy Spirit revealed to him "the grand truth that we are one with Jesus. It isn't necessary to battle, to struggle to have faith, it is enough to rest in Him who is Faithful ...."[4]

Taylor found strength by abiding in Christ and trusting in the fullness of the Holy Spirit. This would carry him through the many difficult years ahead where, among other things, he had to bury his wife and four children. During the crisis of the Boxer Rebellion, when fifty-eight CIM missionaries and twenty-one children were murdered, Taylor's work continued to bring in new recruits. He concluded his long missionary career as a man of prayer and praise who found his value in a relationship with Christ.

Your Name is in the Book!

Hudson Taylor's crisis can be compared to that of Jesus' disciples. When the Lord sent His followers on a mission, they were quickly overwhelmed by the stresses involved in the excitement of serving, and they soon lost focus. Luke describes how this mission was a practicum in which the disciples were to apply the teachings of their Master (Luke 10:1–23). They went, and were thrilled as people were healed, delivered, and convinced about the truths of the kingdom of God. On their return the disciples gave a glowing report to Jesus, saying, "Lord, even the demons are subject to us in Your name" (v. 17). They were overjoyed that they could perform the same wonders as their Master. This was real ministry, and they had proof!

Jesus responded to the disciples with the sobering words, "I was watching Satan fall from heaven like lightning" (v. 18). He was not surprised by their success because He had given them authority to perform the miracles, but He sounded a warning as well, reminding them that they were focused on the wrong priority. The fact that they could overpower the enemy was not significant even if it could give them confidence. Instead, Jesus urged them to rejoice that their names were recorded in heaven (v. 20).

The disciples did not totally understand this concept. Hadn't they just returned from a successful campaign in which they had seen themselves do some pretty amazing stuff? And here He was, telling them to rejoice because their names were written in heaven! Little did they realize that Jesus was trying to teach them two important ministry principles.

Principle 1: Belonging supersedes doing

Jesus taught that through the experiences of life, we must focus on our identity in Him. The disciples were excited that they too could speak and serve with authority, but Jesus wanted them to focus on the fact that they belonged to Him (Luke 10:20).

Jesus had taught the disciples to abide in Him (John 15), underlining that it is impossible to bear fruit or be productive in ministry otherwise "For apart from Me you can do nothing" (v. 3). Another time, He used the image of a shepherd, telling them, "I am the Good

Shepherd; and I know My own, and My own know Me" (John 10:14).

Jesus' words to His first disciples are equally applicable to us. The Scriptures describe at least three personal habits that will increase our sense of belonging to Him.

A. We must make it a habit to meditate on His Word. Our understanding of the Word of God will deepen our commitment to abiding in Him. The Scriptures ask us to meditate on the Word "day and night" (Ps. 1:2). As the palmist affirmed, "I have rejoiced in the way of Thy testimonies, as much as in all riches. I will meditate on Thy precepts" (Ps. 119:14–15).

Hudson Taylor read the Bible through forty times in as many years. A young missionary I know proudly informed his African mentor that he followed this habit, to which the older Christian responded, "I've been reading it two or three times a year for years." That was when the missionary realized that the old man could be found reading his Bible in every spare moment. The example of the elderly man is a reproof to those of us who we are too busy doing mission work to attend to personal growth.

B. We must make it a habit to pray knowingly. The Lord promised: "Call on Me, and I will answer you, and I will tell you great and mighty things, which you do not know" (Jer. 33:3). We know the importance of prayer, but in this context, I would remind us of the truth that "those who wait for the Lord will gain new strength" (Is. 40:31). The Apostle Paul exhorts us to devote ourselves to prayer, "keeping alert in it with an attitude of thanksgiving" (Col. 4:2). In a world with many distractions, we can use a prayer list to focus our attention on the Lord. We can also develop accountability prayer-partner relationships with local believers, missionary colleagues, or roommates. Having only one or two partners will guarantee the intimacy and keep the prayers from becoming words uttered by rote.

C. We must make it a habit to know Him better. The Apostle Paul had every reason to use his pedigree as an excuse for boasting. If anyone had reason to be proud of his achievements, Paul did, but he confessed that he considered them as nothing compared to "the surpassing value" of knowing Christ Jesus, counting them "but rubbish" in order to "gain Christ" (Phil. 3:7–8). He advised his spiritual son, Timothy, to be diligent to present himself "approved to God as a workman who does not need to be ashamed, handling accurately the word of truth" (2 Tim. 2:15). Paul knew that as people know Jesus better, they will "walk in the same manner as He walked" (1 John 2:6).

Most of us know men and women of God who, as they deepen their knowledge of Jesus, become more like Him in their attitudes and action. It was often said that George Müller came from his prayer room shining with the radiance of Jesus. Paul's prayer for his churches was that the believers would be filled with the knowledge of God's will so that they would "walk in a manner worthy of the Lord ... increasing in the knowledge of God" (Col. 1:9–10). How many believers today pay for this knowledge with their blood like the early Christians? Those who do so have discovered that "to live is Christ, and to die is gain" (Phil. 1:21).

If you know Jesus intimately, you will have a dependable refuge during the difficult times. Your private moments with Jesus become opportunities for you to renew your strength, and prayer times can also be the one unchanging feature in your family's schedule. Missionary kids (MKs) understand the trauma of cultural ambiguity. They feel the constant stress of living cross-culturally. When they are young, they need the reassurance that one relationship will not change with every move. The family altar where parents and children take time for prayer, reflection, and discussion will become a child's place of refuge. MKs are known to find stability in this ritual where they always encounter Christ.

Apart from disciplined Bible study, the writings of authors like Richard Foster, A. W. Tozer, Frank Laubach, David Brainard, John Eldredge, and others will help you to know Christ better. Most missionary biographies also give insight into how others have walked with Jesus in a cross-cultural setting. Study the lives of these men and women of God, and learn to walk your road by the light of their experiences.

It is also essential to seek occasional moments of extended prayer and worship in one's mother tongue. Even though you may have become fluent in a language of your hosts, your heart language will always reach deeper into your soul. Worshiping from time to time in this language will strengthen your spiritual conviction and open doors for insights that might not come through a foreign language.

Principle 2: Belonging produces doing

Flushed with success, the disciples felt confident in their ability to do ministry, which in itself is not wrong. Jesus was not surprised that demons had obeyed the disciples, and His reprimand was gentle but clear: "I have given you authority" (Luke 10:19). He wanted them to understand that what they had done was not indicative of their abilities but flowed directly out of who they were in Him. On another occasion, Jesus showed the disciples that they had been unable to heal the epileptic boy because they had not yet learned that He was the source from which their performance would come (Matt. 17:9–21). They had failed because of their "little faith." Out of being comes the fruit of ministry because "he who abides in Me and I in him, bears much fruit...." (John 15:5). Rivers of life-giving water will flow out of our inner being only when we "come ... drink ... and believe" (John 7:37–39).

Mission training programs teach us that we are sent to communicate the good news so that communities of believers are formed. The emerging church built as a result of our service is the evidence that we are fulfilling God's calling, and the number of souls won to Christ indicates that we are not idle and lends credibility to our vocation. But how do we respond when the results don't come quickly? The periods that seem unproductive are when the enemy plants the seeds of doubt, and we hear these thoughts:

"How can you claim God's call on your life when He knows you don't have results to show?"

"God doesn't desire that any perish, but you are letting people perish. Look at them go!"

"Jesus did not call you to live with such carnal believers!"

"Do you think that the Holy Spirit wants you to waste your time with these difficult, unproductive coworkers?"

Usually, the enemy will relate your discouragement to visible results. As persecution, opposition, illness, and other hardships mount, your focus may shift from who you are in Christ to what you need to accomplish for Him, and eventually you wonder, "Was I called to *this*?"

David Brainard saw a people movement to Christ among the indigenous populations of the eastern American colonies, but his success was preceded by three years of difficult and lonely service. Adoniram Judson labored for six years in Burma before seeing his first convert, and Robert Morrison had to spend eight years in China for the same result. In some countries, sent-ones faithfully sowed for fifty years with minuscule results until the tide came in and people turned to Christ in masses. How did these missionaries survive the drought?

The following steps will help you maintain a balance between who you are in Christ and what you do for Him. These steps are based on the presupposition that you follow the first principle of being in Christ.

A. Be committed to personal relationship priorities. Manage that delicate balance in your personal priorities. The Apostle Paul frequently exhorted early churches to remain in Christ and seek to know Him better (Phil. 3:8–10; Col. 2:6). After our relationship with Christ, we must be committed to learning to know ourselves and then relating well with our spouse and children (if any), with our extended family, and with our intimate friends or accountability partners. Each relationship must be kept in its proper place. The danger is that the enemy wants us to become more committed to one relationship than to the others, but we must use discernment and not allow him to throw us off balance.

For example, cross-cultural ambiguity combined with an unhealthy focus on the family can jeopardize our sense of balance. People caught in this cycle will emphasize the needs of family to the exclusion of ministry opportunities. In some cases, children's needs cause a fear-driven anxiety that paralyzes one's commitments to ministry. Then there are those who so fear failure at work that they will sacrifice the stability of the family, allowing their home to become a dizzy center of ministry activity. In both these extreme cases, the enemy has won the battle by throwing life out of kilter. It is usually only a matter of time before the sent-one quits.

B. *Prioritize ministry involvement to your unique spiritual gifts and training.* The Scriptures teach that we are "created in Christ Jesus for good works, which God prepared beforehand, that we should walk in them" (Eph. 2:10), and Jesus said that we are to let our light shine in such a way that people would our good works and glorify our Father in heaven (Matt. 5:16). We have been created redeemed so that our activity will bring people into a relationship with the heavenly Father. With this goal in mind, we must realize that the assembly of believers functions like the human body, with each member having a role to perform (1 Cor. 12:12). Spiritual gifts (*charismata*) have been given to this body by the Holy Spirit, according to His will, to equip its members for works of service, which build up of the body of Christ (Eph. 4:12). Each Christian has a function and has been endowed with the ability to perform it.

Two suggestions will help you prepare for cross-cultural ministry, and they might make your service joyful. First, discover and practice your gift before leaving for your new place of ministry. Sharpening your spiritual gifts and practicing them while in your cultural comfort zone will give you confidence in service before landing amidst strangers and experiencing the insecurity that this can bring. In addition, it will help you to be patient with the seemingly endless task of cross-cultural adjustment. As a sent-one, you already face self-doubt. Language study, in particular, can be very humbling, but with the previous assurance of your skills, you will more quickly find your place of service in your new setting.

Second, learn to be flexible with your talent. Some workers are afraid of the unknown that entering a new culture throws them into a mode of rigidity. They insist that they can only serve in a predetermined way, and this protective mechanism locks their emotions and damages their relationships. If we are confident of our place in Christ, we will more easily face the unknown and learn to exercise our skills in ways that benefit our hosts. Flexibility will release you from binding fear and enable you to serve from a place of peace.

C. *Focus ministry activities on relationship building.* We are exhorted throughout the Scripture to carefully develop relationships with the non-Christian world, with other believers, and with our fellow workers. Paul exhorts us to conduct ourselves with wisdom toward outsiders, making the most of every opportunity (Col. 4:5), and John tells us that if we walk in the light as Jesus is in the light, we will have fellowship with one another (1 John 1:7). There is a connection between our walk with Jesus and the effect it has on others. Our Lord commanded us to love each other "just as I have loved you" (John 15:12), and this is our example for relationship building. The writer to of the letter to the Hebrews reminds us to not stop meeting together, and to encourage one another (Heb. 10:25), and Paul exhorts us to bear one another's burdens and thus fulfill the law of Christ (Gal. 6:2). Every letter of Paul's contains teaching about relationships, and two of the most famous passages are Romans 12:9–16 and Colossians 3:13–16.

As you become involved in serving the new culture and its people, you will develop lasting relations. You will learn to empathize with those who still seek Christ, and you will establish friendships with your neighbors. You will choose to focus on people not projects, and this will help you reach into the community of people seeking Jesus. As they come to Christ, you will deepen your friendship by helping them to walk as Jesus did (Col. 2:6–7).

D. Apply Jesus' authority to your daily walk. Jesus sent His disciples with authority in His name, empowering them to do battle with the enemy, and He later gave them the Supreme Order to make disciples, confirming that all authority in heaven and earth had been given to Him (Matt. 28:18). Do not forget who sent you and against whom you battle. When persecution, illness, or opposition attacks your family, "put on[5] the full armor of God that you may be able to stand firm against the schemes of the devil" (Eph. 6:11). When troubles come, be sure to identify the real enemy. You may be feeling the pressure of the expectations of others, but before lashing out at them, be sure to hear God's Word, His Spirit, and seek wise counsel. Your focus must remain on abiding in Christ.

The Crisis Clarifies the Future

The challenge of the twenty-first century is not to find a better way to reach more people. The real challenge for us is to be men and women who so effectively demonstrate Christ's character that those whom we encounter will want what we have. They will want to know Christ because they like what they see of Him in us.

With the increased emphasis on church planting among people of established religions like Islam, Hinduism, and Buddhism, as well as among more recent Postmoderns and New Agers, we have begun engaging the enemy to a greater degree than ever before. The pitch of that battle is increasing, and we will be tempted to focus on the methodology of mission. In the last century, a sent-one could have chosen from many successful methods. Missionaries, pastors, and lay Christians all had their chance to jump on the bandwagon of new methods. These methods varied from crusades and tabernacle evangelism to seeker-sensitive and big-city outreach. Controversies raged over the difference between social and real gospel and fundamental versus orthodox belief. In missions, we discussed the merits of assimilating the church to the mission and separating mission from the national church. We debated about whether to pay evangelists to do what God has called them to do or to convince the church to do it.

Churches have been pressured with concepts of church growth, church management by objective, and spiritual warfare techniques. These approaches had their place and were effective in their own context, but some workers were so taken by the methods that they lost focus on the Message. In his book, *The Cross and Christian Ministry*, Don Carson warns against such faddism:

> Western evangelicalism tends to run through cycles of fads. At the moment, books are pouring off the presses telling us how to plan for success, how "vision" consists in clearly articulated "ministry goals." How the knowledge of detailed profiles of our communities constitutes the key to successful outreach. I am not for a moment suggesting that there is nothing to be learned from such studies.... Of course all of us need to understand the people to whom we minister, and all of us can benefit from small doses of such literature. But massive doses sooner or later dilute the gospel. Ever so subtly, we start to think that success more critically depends on thoughtful sociological analysis than on the gospel; Barna becomes more important than the Bible. We depend on plans, programs, vision statements—but somewhere along the way we have succumbed to the temptation to displace

the foolishness of the cross with the wisdom of strategic planning.... I fear that the cross, without ever being disowned, is constantly in danger of being dismissed from the central place it must enjoy, by relatively peripheral insights that take on far too much weight. Whenever the periphery is in danger of displacing the center, we are not far removed from idolatry.[6]

Conclusion

Several years ago, a professor warned his young students, "The enemy wants you to be off-balance. He either will distract you enough so that you are totally off-center, or he will get you to so concentrate on the center that you will be off on everything else." Few understood the implications of these wise words until they had spent several years in another culture. I know, because I was one of those students.

When we confront the crises of ministry, we realize how easily we can lose focus, and it is in the heat of a crisis that the Holy Spirit will reset our heart on abiding in Christ. The crisis brings us to a decision that will change the direction of our career and it thus becomes a defining moment.

May each of your career-defining crises cause you to know Christ better and lead others to do the same. I pray that the insights and principles in this book will be helpful as you navigate the many decisions of your cross-cultural service.

Appendix A

Check Your Fluency Progress

THIS BASIC CHECKLIST provides a step-by-step measurement for your language learning progress. Summer Institute of Linguistics (SIL) and other professional language training organizations provide detailed material for learning without needing to take a formal program. *Language Acquisition Made Practical* (LAMP) provides a more detailed checklist.

Language Learning Guidelines

A. Statement of philosophy

In one phrase: "learn to *speak* your host language"

- This language study program is aimed at enabling you, the learner, to sufficiently understand the grammar so that you become a fluent speaker.

- The ultimate test of your fluency in this language is that you will be able to clearly and freely communicate with native speakers, and even maintain a conversation with them.

B. Language advisor (LA)

- He or she is usually a mission colleague.

- The advisor should be fluent in the language you plan to learn. If this is not possible, the LA should have learned at least one other foreign language.

The LA's ministry objectives should be:

- To help the Language Learner (LL) establish language- learning goals that lead to oral fluency.

- To help the LL find the proper language helper (LH).

Note: Language helper is the correct term. "Language informant" should not be used as it implies secretive spying activities.

- To encourage the LL to progress toward speaking. This can be done by

   1) Making regular visits to check on progress, discuss problems, etc. (Weekly visits are advised; but visits should not be fewer than one per month.)

   2) Arranging for exams and quick grading of written exams by a native speaker.

   3) Providing accountability for the LL

C. Language learner (LL)

- The LL will, under normal circumstances, complete language study program within the first two years of living among the host people.

- The LL will devote six hours per day (30 hours per week) to language study. This includes time spent study, conversation and listening time in the language.

- The LL should establish an accountability relationship with the LA in order to keep learning progress on schedule.

D. Guidelines for measuring fluency progress

Level 1: Language survivor

Your goal: To speak fluently so you can survive in your new environment.

Time: 3-6 months

Procedure

1) Prepare written dialogues or descriptions in the new language, which will be corrected by the LH. From each dialogue you should collect

      i) new vocabulary

      ii) common grammatical phrases and expressions

      iii) note idioms, customs, and behavior

2) Write the following dialogues with the LH's help. Learn them and memorize them! (See LAMP)

Check each item when you have mastered it

- ❑ Lesson 1: Greeting and leave-taking
- ❑ Lesson 2: Introducing family members
- ❑ Lesson 3: Visiting a friend's house (note names of things in the sitting room and bedroom, etc.)
- ❑ Lesson 4: Eating with a friend (note food names and custom)
- ❑ Lesson 5: Parts of the body (story of kids drawing in the sand)
- ❑ Lesson 6: Parts of the face (continue above story)
- ❑ Lesson 7: Giving directions for travel (includes prepositions)
- ❑ Lesson 8: Shopping (numbers)

3) Grammar to learn in Level 1: Where possible develop fluency drills to memorize the grammatical structures.

- ❑ "I need _____"
- ❑ "I want to ____"
- ❑ "I like (to)_____"
- ❑ imperative (negative and positive)
- ❑ present tenses (negative and positive)
- ❑ conjugation of all new verbs you learned
- ❑ comparison and contrast
- ❑ numbers: ordinal (one, two, etc.) 1-1000
- ❑ cardinal (first, second, third, etc)
- ❑ months, days of the week, time of day
- ❑ begin noting tone and accent

Exam #1: 80 points written, 20 points oral, on grammar forms learned, including greetings, questions about your job, family, and your reason for being here. (*Note:* the oral exam should take between 10 and 12 minutes.)

Level 2: Trader

Your goal: to speak fluently so you can trade ideas, opinions, and feelings, with native speakers.

Time: 3-6 months

Procedure:

1) Prepare written dialogues or scripts that elicit feelings, opinions, and emotions

- ❑ Lesson 9: Child is born (joy, anticipation)
- ❑ Lesson 10: Child is sick (fear, anxiety)
- ❑ Lesson 11: Seeking remedies from feticher, marabou, medicine man, or doctor (anger, doubt)
- ❑ Lesson 12: Food preparation (enjoyment, fulfillment)
- ❑ Lesson 13: Visit hospital (wonder, uncertainty)
- ❑ Lesson 14: Wedding (excitement)
- ❑ Lesson 15: Funeral (sorrow, anguish)
- ❑ Lesson 16: Initiation or a celebration of passage, such as birthday, graduation, first job (accomplishment, honor)
- ❑ Lesson 17: Personal testimony in (7–10 minutes share you came to faith in Christ; practice four times before your Level #2 exam.)
- ❑ Lesson18: Prepare five different prayers that are commonly used. Learn and use them. You will be asked to write one for your exam. Examples: table grace, invocation, offering, pastoral prayer, prayer for healing, encouragement, etc.

2) Grammar: Include this in Level 2 dialogues

- ❑ Learn all remaining tenses, using each successive lesson to develop the connotations of time expression.
- ❑ Learn idiomatic expressions used to express various moods, attitudes, and feelings.

❑ Learn syntax items that make communications smooth: therefore, whereas, so, then, in view of, slowly, quickly, furthermore, etc.

Exam #2: 70 points written: tests grammar forms learned, includes one prayer randomly selected, and a 100 word exposé on a selected topic, 30 points oral explanation of a recent experience describing the feelings and lessons learned. You will share your testimony without notes. (*Note:* Oral exam should take 15-17 minutes.)

Level 3: Storyteller

Your goal: To fluently tell stories and thus communicate ideas and truth so that the native speaker understands.

Time: 3–6 months.

Note: After the Level 2 exam, if you are asked to pray in public or in a home setting, you must do it in your new language; you are now a "storyteller." All conversation with the LH must be in the new language.

Procedure:

1) Prepare written stories with help of the LH or other resources. Learn each of the above stories and practice telling them at least five times each to different native speakers. This need not be a formal setting, but you must tell each parable five times. Try telling it to children, people in the park, friends, and more.

Seven biblical parables

Seven stories from local folklore, or cultural literature

Ten to fifteen one-sentence local proverbs that teach or apply the parables and stories mentioned above.

2) Expand your testimony to a mini-message based on one key passage. Preach it or share it three times using notes, not a manuscript.

3) Memorize seven Bible verses that you use frequently when sharing the gospel with non-Christians.

4) 300 pages of collateral reading in the literature of your people group. It is preferred that this material be in the host language. If nothing is available, reading can be done in your native language.

Read one of the Gospels (or an OT book) in the host language (if the Bible translation is available).

5) Grammar to learn

- ❑   Rhythm and intonation; imitate the music of language
- ❑   Note compound sentences and relative clauses

6) Spend at least seven days in a total language environment (i.e., in a village or urban community where the new language is the principal form of communication). This can be done in two visits of three days or together. But it is the minimum time to help immerse you in the language.

Exam #3: 60 points written: You will be given a fable or history in the language and have to answer discussion questions and prepare an exposé.

40 points oral: You will converse with the LH answering five discussion questions on the exam story narrating one of the parables you learned (randomly chosen). You will also be asked to recite three of the Bible verses learned during this period.

Level 4: Persuader

Your goal: Your aim is to speak with sufficient freedom so that you are able to persuade native speakers to change their opinion or decision about a subject.

Time: 3–6 months

Procedure:

- ❑   Prepare five messages in keeping with the kind of ministry you will have.

Pastor, evangelist—sermons from the Bible

Teacher—lesson plans

Nurse—health lessons

Women's work—Bible, family, etc.

- ❑ Teach each lesson at least once, using only notes (not a manuscript)
- ❑ Spend a minimum of seven days in a total language environment before you take the Level 4 exam.
- ❑ Prepare your final oral presentation with the LH's help to correct errors. The topic should be in keeping with your ministry.
- ❑ Continue Bible reading in the language. Read at least one Gospel or other section of the Bible.

Exam #4: 100 points. For the oral presentation including answering at least five discussion questions posed by a native speaker on aspects of your presentation.

Remember: Your goal is to be a fluent *speaker* of the language! You are entering the adventure of learning *to speak* the language. The more you use it, the faster you will progress.

Appendix B

Evaluating a Church's Maturity

THE PURPOSE OF THIS evaluation tool is (i) to present biblical teaching about the character of the church, and (ii) to motivate church leaders and local believers to take steps that will propel them toward spontaneous growth. This test can be given to individuals or to a group.

Procedure

1. Take the people through a study of key Bible passages that describe the four qualities of the Christ-centered church. This tool helps to focus attention on God's description, not ours.

2. Distribute the procedure to everyone and explain the purpose of the evaluation, emphasizing that the local assembly should seek to conform to God's standard for a Christ-centered focus. It should be clarified that this is not an exam. The test is not a resource of our importance in God's eyes, and the result will not tell us that we are loved more or less by God.

3. Explain that people will respond to each item by choosing one number that most accurately describes their answer to the question.

Note: If a question does not apply to your assembly, it should be left unanswered and the calculation for an average score at the end of the section will be adjusted.

4. When everyone has completed the questions, tabulate the results and mark the average on the scale. A group average is put on the chart to give a picture of the church's maturity.

A score above 2.5 suggests good health, and we must encourage God's people to continue maturing.

A score below 2.5 is a warning that we need to seek improvement. For each low area, follow the next procedure.

5. Review the scores on the chart with the group, allowing participants to express freely their general impressions and reactions to what they see on the chart. Lead them through these four steps

A. What realities in your church caused you to give the lower scores in this section? Give specific examples for each item. Do not accept statements that compare this church against another church.

B. What biblical teaching describes the root cause of these problems?

C. Develop a strategy that will remedy the weakness:

Make a Bible teaching plan that challenges people to mature in this area.

As a group, establish a strategy for training and mentoring church leaders in this teaching, so that the challenge will reach all levels of the Body life.

D) Describe a measurable procedure or goal that will help your group to know that believers are progressing toward maturity.

Assessment Tool

The following questions will help you to assess your congregation as a Christ-centered church. Scores must be given on the basis of the assembly's cultural demands and expectations relating to that item, always keeping your eyes focused on the biblical image of the church while assigning a value for each question as follows:

0 = no activity, incapable of doing it

1 = weak activity, rarely done

2 = below average activity, but functional

3 = active, average quality

4 = habitual activity, strong

5 = very active, strong, alive

1. Worship and giving

The Church demonstrates love for God with a whole heart, soul, and strength by the habits of worship and giving (Deut. 6:4–5; Rom. 12:1–2; 2 Cor. 8:2, 8, 14; Col. 3:16–17; Eph. 5:18–20).

1. There is a regular habitual time of worship

0 — 1 — 2 — 3 — 4 — 5

2. Cell groups (small groups) worship consistently

0 — 1 — 2 — 3 — 4 — 5

3. Most believers participate in worship activities

0 — 1 — 2 — 3 — 4 — 5

4. Worship time, in large of small groups, demonstrates orderliness and discipline

0 — 1 — 2 — 3 — 4 — 5

5. Worship time follows a pattern consistent with NT example of worship content including scripture reading, hymns, prayers, study, giving, teaching, and exhortation

0 — 1 — 2 — 3 — 4 — 5

6. Believers demonstrate attitudes of respect, humility, joy, love, etc. in worship

0 — 1 — 2 — 3 — 4 — 5

7. Songs and praise are consistent with biblical truth in a culturally understood form

0 — 1 — 2 — 3 — 4 — 5

8. All believers are taught and encouraged to exercise their spiritual gifts

0 — 1 — 2 — 3 — 4 — 5

9. Teaching and preaching is biblical in content

0 — 1 — 2 — 3 — 4 — 5

10. The Lord's Supper is celebrated regularly

0 — 1 — 2 — 3 — 4 — 5

11. Baptism is practiced at regular intervals (2-3 times annually)

0 — 1 — 2 — 3 — 4 — 5

12. Believers consistently give freely and joyfully of personal wealth and possession

0 — 1 — 2 — 3 — 4 — 5

13. Believers financially support their pastor and church leaders, according to cultural norms

0 — 1 — 2 — 3 — 4 — 5

14. Leaders practice financial accountability

0 — 1 — 2 — 3 — 4 — 5

15. Worshipers complete their time of praise and prayer with the conviction that they have met with God.

0 — 1 — 2 — 3 — 4 — 5

Total: _____

Divide by 15 to get the average score: _____

2. Witness and mission

The church actively shares Christ, by conduct and word, with those who do not know Christ as Savior (Matt. 9:36; 28:18–20; Acts 13:1–12).

1. All believers are encouraged to share their faith through their life-walk

0 — 1 — 2 — 3 — 4 — 5

2. Believers are trained in personal evangelism

0 — 1 — 2 — 3 — 4 — 5

3. Personal evangelism occurs spontaneously outside of worship settings

0 — 1 — 2 — 3 — 4 — 5

4. People often spend time praying for their non-Christian relatives and friends

0 — 1 — 2 — 3 — 4 — 5

5. The arrival of new converts is often discussed in the assembly

0 — 1 — 2 — 3 — 4 — 5

6. New converts are quickly connected to a small group
0 — 1 — 2 — 3 — 4 — 5

7. New converts are integrated into the assembly
0 — 1 — 2 — 3 — 4 — 5

8. Believers, as a group, faithfully demonstrate holiness and godliness in conduct
0 — 1 — 2 — 3 — 4 — 5

9. Believers have a good reputation in the community
0 — 1 — 2 — 3 — 4 — 5

10. Evangelism/mission to unreached people is promoted regularly in the assembly
0 — 1 — 2 — 3 — 4 — 5

11. Evangelists/missionaries are sent from the local assembly to establish other groups of believers among unreached ethnic groups
0 — 1 — 2 — 3 — 4 — 5

12. The assembly organizes its program for supporting and sending evangelists and missionaries
0 — 1 — 2 — 3 — 4 — 5

13. Evangelistic/missionary efforts result in new cells of believers being planted   0 — 1 — 2 — 3 — 4 — 5

14. The assembly supports cross-cultural training programs for its sent-ones
0 — 1 — 2 — 3 — 4 — 5

15. The assembly seeks ways to meet social needs of the community as a demonstration of its love for God
0 — 1 — 2 — 3 — 4 — 5

Total: _____

Divide by 15 to get the average score: _____

3. Teaching and training

The Church is motivated to grow and mature spiritually by the teaching of God's Word (Matt. 28:19; Acts 2:42; Col. 2:6–; 2 Tim. 2:14–26).

1. New believers are quickly directed into teaching settings for new converts   0 — 1 — 2 — 3 — 4 — 5

2. New believers are associated with mature followers, who will mentor them into active fellowship

0 — 1 — 2 — 3 — 4 — 5

3. Believers are taught biblical principles of stewardship of their wealth

0 — 1 — 2 — 3 — 4 — 5

4. The meaning and importance of baptism are taught regularly (twice per year)   0 — 1 — 2 — 3 — 4 — 5

5. Regular programs of instruction are provided for all age groups   0 — 1 — 2 — 3 — 4 — 5

6. Youth programs include Bible study, teaching, and music
0 — 1 — 2 — 3 — 4 — 5

7. Literacy programs (where needed) are organized and operated by the local assembly

0 — 1 — 2 — 3 — 4 — 5

8. Leadership training is encouraged for emerging leaders at all levels   0 — 1 — 2 — 3 — 4 — 5

9. Believers are encouraged to become involved in teaching and training ministries

0 — 1 — 2 — 3 — 4 — 5

10. Training enables believers to participate in local ministries
0 — 1 — 2 — 3 — 4 — 5

11. A consistent teacher training program is developing a corps of Bible teachers   0 — 1 — 2 — 3 — 4 — 5

12. Students in training are supported financially, and spiritually, by their sending assembly

0 — 1 — 2 — 3 — 4 — 5

13. Leaders completing training are integrated into ministry roles appropriate to their spiritual gifts

0 — 1 — 2 — 3 — 4 — 5

14. Bible teaching literature is available and used in the teaching ministries

0 — 1 — 2 — 3 — 4 — 5

15. Christian discipline is practiced to restore disobedient followers to Christ

0 — 1 — 2 — 3 — 4 — 5

Total: _____

Divide by 15 to get the average score: _____

4. Leading and serving

The Church is organized to effectively serve others through the use local human and material resources. (Matt. 18:15–20; Rom. 12:3-21; Gal. 6:1–5; Eph. 4:11–18; Col. 1:18; 1 Pet. 5:1-6; Jude 20–24).

1. Leaders are chosen or appointed according to biblical criteria, in a culturally understood manner (Acts 6:1–6; 1 Tim. 4; Titus 1)

0 — 1 — 2 — 3 — 4 — 5

2. Local leaders make decisions for their local assembly or communities   0 — 1 — 2 — 3 — 4 — 5

3. Local leaders put into action these decisions

0 — 1 — 2 — 3 — 4 — 5

4. Decision making follows a culturally acceptable procedure

0 — 1 — 2 — 3 — 4 — 5

5. Leaders see themselves as accountable to God

0 — 1 — 2 — 3 — 4 — 5

6. Leaders perceive themselves as accountable to their people

0 — 1 — 2 — 3 — 4 — 5

7. The people respect and follow their leaders, seeing them as divinely appointed

$$0 — 1 — 2 — 3 — 4 — 5$$

8. The assembly encourages local emerging leaders

$$0 — 1 — 2 — 3 — 4 — 5$$

9. Youth are encouraged to take leadership roles as their gifts emerge $\qquad 0 — 1 — 2 — 3 — 4 — 5$

10. Youth are sent and supported in leadership training and education, including Bible schools, TEE, etc.

$$0 — 1 — 2 — 3 — 4 — 5$$

11. Elders delegate responsibilities to emerging leaders

$$0 — 1 — 2 — 3 — 4 — 5$$

12. Leadership roles are patterned upon Jesus' model of a servant (John 13)

$$0 — 1 — 2 — 3 — 4 — 5$$

13. Leaders and believers follow biblical procedures for discipline $\qquad 0 — 1 — 2 — 3 — 4 — 5$

14. When restoring a disobedient leader, the same biblical criteria applies to leaders as to the congregation

$$0 — 1 — 2 — 3 — 4 — 5$$

15. The local church's organizational structure is financially supported by its members

$$0 — 1 — 2 — 3 — 4 — 5$$

Total: _____

Divide by 15 to get the average score: _____

Visualizing Your Progress

	Worship & Giving	Evangelism & Missions	Teaching & Training	Leading & Serving
5				
4				
3				
2				
1				

Note: This assessment does not determine whether an assembly is really a church. It only indicates the health of the church, showing areas of strength and weakness.

Additional Reading

THE FOLLOWING RESOURCES will deepen your understanding of the principal subject of each chapter or section. These selections have been made according to subject. In some cases, a title may be repeated in another chapter to indicate valued information for that subject.

Chapter 1

Bonk, Jonathan J. *Missions and Money: Affluence as a Western Missionary Problem.* Maryknoll: Orbis, 1991.

Christian, Carol, and Gladys Plummer. *God and One Red Head: Mary Slessor of Calabar.* Grand Rapids: Zondervan, 1970.

Coleman, Robert E. *The Great Commission Life-Style.* Grand Rapids: Revell/Baker, 1992.

Elmer, Duane. *Cross-Cultural Connections: Stepping Out and Fitting in around the World.* Downers Grove: IVP, 2002.

Foyle, Marjory F. *Overcoming Missionary Stress.* Wheaton: EMIS, 1987.

Hiebert, Paul G., and Eloise Hiebert Menneses. *Incarnational Ministry: Planting Churches in Band, Tribal, Peasant, and Urban Societies.* Grand Rapids: Baker, 1995.

Hufman, Samuel. *Mission Work in Today's World: Insights and Outlook.* Pasadena: William Carey Library, 1992.

Keidel, Levi O., Jr. *Conflict or Connection: Interpersonal Relationships in Cross-Cultural Settings.* Carol Stream: EMIS, 1996.

Lingenfelter, Sherwood G., and Marvin K. Mayers. *Ministering Cross-Culturally.* Grand Rapids: Baker, 1986.

Loss, Myron. *Culture Shock: Dealing with Stress in Cross-Cultural Living.* Winona Lake: Light and Life Press, 1985.

Miller, Basel. *Mary Slessor: Heroine of Calabar.* Minneapolis: Bethany House, 1974.

Smalley, William A., ed. *Readings in Missionary Anthropology II.* Pasadena: William Carey Library, 1978.

Chapter 2

Brewster, Thomas and Elizabeth. *Language Acquisition Made Practical.* Pasadena: Lingua House, 1976.

Common European Framework of Reference for Languages: Learning, Teaching, Assessment. Cambridge: Cambridge Press. <www.coe.int//T/E/cultural_co-operation/education/languages/>

Davidson, Norman J. *Moffat of Africa.* New York: George H. Doran, 1926.

Larson, Donald. *Guidelines for Barefoot Language Learning.* St. Paul: CMS Publishing, 1984.

Larson, Donald N., and William A. Smalley. *Becoming Bilingual: A Guide to Language Learning.* Pasadena: William Carey Library, 1972.

Loss, Myron. *Culture Shock: Dealing with Stress in Cross-Cultural Living.* Winona Lake: Light and Life Press, 1985.

Smalley, William A., ed. *Readings in Missionary Anthropology II.* Pasadena: William Carey Library, 1978.

Smith, E. W. *Robert Moffat: One of God's Gardeners.* London: Lutterworth, 1952.

Winitz, Harris. *Learnables,* Vols.1–4. Kansas City: International Linguistics, 1990.

Chapter 3

Allen, E. Anthony. *Caring for the Whole Person.* Monrovia: MARC, 1995.

Allen, Roland. *Missionary Methods: St. Paul's or Ours?* Grand Rapids: Eerdmans, 1972.

Bunch, Roland. *Two Ears of Corn: A Guide to People-Centered Agricultural Improvement*. Oklahoma City: World Neighbors, 1982.

Cheyne, John R. *International Agents: A Guide to Developmental Ministries*. Monrovia: MARC, 1998.

Elliston, Edgar J. *Christian Relief and Development: Developing Workers for Effective Ministry*. Dallas: Word, 1989.

Evans, David, Ronald I. Vos, and Keith P. Wright. *Biblical Holism and Agriculture*. Pasadena: William Carey Library, 2003.

McAlpine, Thomas H. *By Word, Work and Wonder*. Monrovia: MARC, 1995.

Olasky, Marvin. *The Tragedy of American Compassion*. Wheaton: Crossway, 1992.

Paton, John. *Thirty Years with South Sea Cannibals: Autobiography of John G. Paton*. Chicago: Moody, 1964.

Ram, Eric, ed. *Transforming Health: Christian Approaches to Health and Healing*. Monrovia: MARC, 1995.

Stott, John R. W. *Christian Mission in the Modern World*. London: IVP, 1976.

Van Geest, William. "Development and other religious activities." *Together,* 55 (July-September 1997), 4.

Wetmore, Gordon. *A Contemporary View of the Book of Acts and Its Relationship to People in Need or Little Ones to Him Belong* in AERDO Occasional Paper # 1. Washington, D.C: AERDO, n.d.

Chapter 4

Allen, Roland. *Missionary Methods: St. Paul's or Ours?* Grand Rapids: Eerdmans, 1962.

Bharati, Dayanand. *Living Water and Indian Bowl*. Pasadena: William Carey Library, 2004.

Downs, Tim. *Finding Common Ground*. Chicago: Moody, 1999.

Green, Michael. *Evangelism in the Early Church*. Grand Rapids: Eerdmans, 1970.

Hesselgrave, David. *Communicating Christ Cross-Culturally.* Grand Rapids: Zondervan, 1978.

_____. *Planting Churches Cross-Culturally.* Grand Rapids: Baker, 1983.

Hile, Pat. "Communicating the Gospel in Terms of Felt Need." *Missiology*, 5:4 (October 1977), 499–506.

Lim, David, and Steven Spaulding, eds. *Sharing Jesus in the Buddhist World.* Pasadena: William Carey Library, 2003.

Lingenfelter, Sherwood G., and Marvin K. Mayers. *Ministering Cross-Culturally: An Incarnational Model for Personal Relationships.* Grand Rapids: Baker, 1986.

Chapter 5

Engel, James F. *How to Communicate the Gospel Effectively.* Achimota, Ghana: African Christian Press, 1988.

Gregory, John Milton. *The Seven Laws of Teaching.* Grand Rapids: Baker, 1967.

Livingstone, Greg. *Planting Churches in Muslim Cities: A Team Approach.* Grand Rapids: Baker, 1993.

McGavran, Donald. *The Bridges of God.* New York: Friendship Press, 1955.

_____. *Understanding Church Growth.* Grand Rapids: Eerdmans, 1970.

Miller, Paul. *Group Dynamics in Evangelism.* Scottsdale: Herald, 1958.

Pickett, J. W., A. L. Warnshuis, G. H. Singh, and D. A. McGavran. *Church Growth and Group Conversion.* Pasadena: William Carey Library, 1973.

Richard, H. L. "Is Extraction Evangelism Still the Way to Go?" *Mission Frontiers Bulletin,* 18:9–10 (September-October 1996), 15.

_____. *Following Jesus in the Hindu Context.* Pasadena: William Carey Library, 1999.

Stott, John R. W. *Christian Mission in the Modern World.* Downers Grove: IVP, 1976.

Chapters 6–8

Allen, Roland. *Missionary Methods: St. Paul's or Ours?* Grand Rapids: Eerdmans, 1972.

_____. *Spontaneous Expansion of the Church.* London: World Dominion, 1962.

Ayers, Francis O. *The Ministry of the Laity.* Philadelphia: Westminister, 1962.

Berg, Mike, and Paul Pretiz. *Spontaneous Combustion: Grass Roots Christianity Latin American Style.* Pasadena: William Carey Library, 1996.

Bosch, David. *Transforming Mission.* Maryknoll: Orbis, 1991.

Carson, D. A., ed. *Right with God: Justification in the Bible and the World.* Grand Rapids: Baker, 1992, 216–255.

_____, ed. *The Church in the Bible and the World: An International Study.* Grand Rapids: Baker, 1987, 13–212.

Clark, J. W. Sidney. *The Indigenous Church.* London: World Dominion, 1923.

Fortunato, Frank. "An Army of Artists." *Mission Frontiers Bulletin,* 18:5–8 (May-August 1996), 20.

_____. "The Worship and Arts Resource Network." *Mission Frontiers Bulletin,* 18:5–8 (May-August 1996), 18.

_____. "Trends in Global Worship." *Mission Frontiers Bulletin* 18:5–8 (May-August 1996), 24.

Gable, Phillip. *Everything You Need to Know to Grow a Messianic Synagogue.* Pasadena: William Carey Library, 1974.

Green, Michael. *Evangelism in the Early Church.* Grand Rapids: Eerdmans, 1970.

Hall, Dave. "Taking Worship to the Nations." *Mission Frontiers Bulletin,* 18:5–8 (May-August 1996), 28.

Hayford, Jack. *Mastering Worship.* Portland: Multnomah, 1990.

Hesselgrave, David. *Communicating Christ Cross-Culturally.* Grand Rapids: Zondervan, 1978.

_____, ed. *Dynamic Religious Movements: Case Studies in Growing Religious Movements in Various Cultures.* Grand Rapids: Baker, 1978.

_____. *Today's Choices for Tomorrow's Mission.* Grand Rapids: Zondervan, 1988.

_____, and Edward Rommen. *Contextualization: Meanings, Methods and Models.* Grand Rapids: Baker, 1992.

Hodges, Catherine. "The Batak Heresy: The Struggle to Achieve Meaningful Worship." *Mission Frontiers Bulletin,* 18:5–8 (May-August 1996), 16.

Hodges, Melvin L. *The Indigenous Church: A Complete Handbook on how to Grow Young Churches.* Springfield, MO: Gospel Publishing House, 1976.

Kraft, C. H., and T. N. Wisely, eds. *Readings in Dynamic Indigeneity.* Pasadena: William Carey Library, 1979.

Lingenfelter, Judith E. and Sherwood G. *Teaching Cross-Culturally.* Grand Rapids: Baker, 2003.

Livingstone, Greg. *Planting Churches in Muslim Cities.* Grand Rapids: Baker, 1993.

Parshall, Phil. *New Paths in Muslim Evangelism.* Grand Rapids: Baker, 1995.

Petersen, Jim. *Church Without Walls: Moving Beyond Traditional Boundaries.* Colorado Springs: NavPress, 1992.

Piper, John. "The Supremacy of God in Missions Through Worship." *Mission Frontiers Bulletin,* 18:5–8 (May-August 1996), 9.

Popjes, Jack. "Music to Their Ears: An Ethnomusicologist Helps the Canelas of Brazil Worship More Meaningfully." *Mission Frontiers Bulletin,* 18:5-8 (May-August 1996), 15.

Radcliff, Lawrence. "A Field Worker Speaks out About the Rush to Reach all Peoples." *Mission Frontiers Bulletin,* 20:1–2 (January-February 1998), 40–47.

Read, William R., Victor M. Monterrosa, and Harmon A. Johnson. *Latin American Church Growth.* Grand Rapids: Eerdmans, 1969.

Richards, Lawrence. *A Theology of Christian Education.* Grand Rapids: Zondervan, 1975.

Snyder, Howard A. *The Community of the King.* Madison: IVP, 1977.

_____. *The Problem of Wineskins: Church Structure in a Technological Age.* Madison: IVP, 1975.

Subbamma, B. V. *New Patterns for Discipling Hindus.* Pasadena: William Carey Library, 1970.

Wagner, C. Peter. *Look Out! The Pentecostals are Coming.* Carol Stream: Creation House, 1973.

Wardle, Terry. *Exalt Him: Designing Dynamic Worship Services.* Harrisburg: Christian Publications, 1988.

Webber, Robert. *Celebrating our Faith: Evangelism Through Worship.* New York: Harper and Row, 1986.

Chapters 9–10

Beyerhaus, Peter, and Henry Lefever. *The Responsible Church and the Foreign Mission.* Grand Rapids: Eerdmans, 1964.

Bridges, William. *Transitions: Making Senses of Life's Changes.* Philippines: Addison-Wesley, 1980.

Bush, Luis, and Lorry Lutz. *Partners in Ministry: The Direction of World Evangelism.* Downers Grove: IVP, 1990.

Cole, Edwin Louis. *Facing the Challenge of Crisis and Change.* Tulsa: Honor Books, 1993.

Fetherlin, Robert. *Transition that Enables the Church to Stand Strong: The Changing Relationship in the Work of the Christian & Missionary Alliance in Africa.* D.Miss. dissertation. Deerfield: Trinity International University, 1998.

Fraser, David J. *The Church in New Frontiers for Mission.* Monrovia: MARC, 1983.

Fuller, W. Harold. *Mission-Church Dynamics: How to Change Bicultural Tensions into Dynamic Missionary Outreach.* Pasadena: William Carey Library, 1980.

Kraakevik, James H., and Dotsey Wellwer, eds. *Partners in the Gospel.* Wheaton: Billy Graham Center, 1992.

Neill, Stephen. *Creative Tension.* London: Edinburgh House Press, 1959.

Steffen, Tom A. *Passing the Baton: Church Planting that Empowers.* La Habra: Center for Organizational and Ministry Development, 1993.

_____. *Planned Phase-Out: A Checklist for Cross-Cultural Church Planters.* San Francisco: Austin and Winfield, 1992.

Taylor, William D., ed. *Kingdom Partnership for Synergy in Mission.* Pasadena: William Carey Library, 1994.

Venn, Henry. *To Apply the Gospel.* Grand Rapids: Eerdmans, 1971.

Chapter 11

Allen, Roland. *Missionary Methods: St. Paul's or Ours?* Grand Rapids: Eerdmans, 1972.

_____. *Spontaneous Expansion of the Church.* London: World Dominion, 1962.

Baaben, A. Abu. *African Perspectives on Colonialism.* Baltimore: John Hopkins Press, 1987.

Batchelor, Peter. *People in Rural Development.* Carlisle, UK: Paternoster Press, 1981.

Bharati, Dayanand. *Living Water and Indian Bowl.* Pasadena: William Carey Library, 2004.

Bonk, Jonathan. *Missions and Money: Affluence as a Western Missionary Problem.* Maryknoll: Orbis, 1991.

Kabou, Axelle. *Et si l'Afrique réfusait le developpement?* Paris: Harmattan, 1991.

Kornfield, William J. "What hath our Western Money and our Western Gospel Wrought?" *Mission Frontiers Bulletin,* 19:1–2 (January-February 1997), 19.

Museveni, Yoweri K. *What is Africa's Problem?* Kampala, Uganda: NRM Publications, 1992.

Rickette, Donald. *Building Strategic Relationships.* Enumclaw: Winepress Publications, 2003.

Roy, Frank L. "Proceed with Caution." *Mission Frontiers Bulletin,* 19:1–2 (January-February 1997), 21.

Schwartz, Glenn. *Selected Writings.* Reading, UK: World Mission Associates.[1]

_____. "From Dependency to Fulfillment." *Evangelical Missions Quarterly,* 273 (July 1991), 218–221.

_____. "It's Time to Get Serious About the Cycle of Dependence in Africa." *Evangelical Missions Quarterly,* 29:2 (April 1993), 126–130.

_____. "Cutting the Apron Strings" *Evangelical Missions Quarterly,* 30:1 (January 1994), 36–43.

Shorter, Aylward. *African Theology: Adaptation or Incarnation?* Maryknoll: Orbis, 1977.

Tippett, Alan R. *Verdict Theology in Missionary Theory.* Lincoln: Lincoln Christian College Press, 1969.

Wakatama, Pius. *Independence of the Third World Church: An African's Perspective on Missionary Work.* Downers Grove: IVP, 1976.

Chapter 12

Eldredge, John. *The Journey of Desire.* Nashville: Thomas Nelson, 2000.

_____. *Wild at Heart.* Nashville: Thomas Nelson, 2001.

Foster, Richard. *Celebration of Discipline.* San Francisco: Harper and Row, 1978.

_____. *Freedom of Simplicity.* San Francisco: Harper and Row, 1981.

Foyle, Marjory F. *Overcoming Missionary Stress.* Wheaton: EMIS, 1987.

Hughes, Kent and Barbara. *Liberating Ministry from the Success Syndrome.* Wheaton: Tyndale House, 1982.

Keidel, Levi. *Conflict or Connection.* Wheaton: EMIS, 1997.

Lannon, Jack. *Untapped Potential: Turning Ordinary People into Extraordinary Performers.* Nashville: Thomas Nelson, 1998.

MacDonald, Gordon. *Ordering Your Private World.* Nashville: Thomas Nelson, 1985.

O'Donnell, Kelley, ed. *Doing Member Care Well.* Pasadena: William Carey Library, 2002.

Packer, J. I. *Knowing God.* Downers Grove: IVP, 1973.

Piper, John. *Let the Nations be Glad!* Grand Rapids: Baker, 1993.

Swenson, Richard A. *Margin: Restoring Emotional, Physical, Financial, and Time Reserves to Overloaded Lives.* Colorado Springs: NavPress, 1992.

Taylor, Howard. *Hudson Taylor and the China Inland Mission.* London: China Inland Mission, 1958.

Taylor, Howard and Mary. *Hudson Taylor's Spiritual Secret.* Chicago: Moody, 1987.

Tozer, A. W. *An Anthology.* Harrisburg: Christian Publications, 1984.

_____. *The Best of A. W. Tozer.* Grand Rapids: Baker, 1978.

_____. *The Knowledge of the Holy.* New York: Harper and Row, 1961.

_____. *The Pursuit of God.* Harrisburg: Christian Publications, 1993.

Notes

Introduction

[1] Message is capitalized, to distinguish the Truth that Christ asks us to tell from other messages that may contain truth, but may not necessarily be what we are sent to proclaim. Story and Truth are also be capitalized to clarify this difference.

[2] The verses for this collage have been taken from the New International Version.

[3] The gerund form more correctly expresses the tense of the verb.

Chapter 1

[1] Ruth Tucker, *From Jerusalem to Irian Jaya* (Grand Rapids: Zondervan, 1983), 158–163.

[2] Elizabeth Isichei, *A History of Christianity in Africa: From Antiquity to the Present* (London: SPCK, 1995), 176.

[3] Jonathan J. Bonk, *Missions and Money: Affluence as a Western Missionary Problem* (Maryknoll: Orbis, 1991), 1, 16.

Chapter 2

[1] C. Northcott, *Robert Moffat: Pioneer in Africa 1817–1870* (London: Lutterworth, 1961).

[2] Carl F. Keil and Franz Delitzsch, *Keil and Delitzsch Old Testament Commentaries* 6 vols. (Grand Rapids: A P & P, n.d.), 1:49.

[3] Louis Berkhoff, *Systematic Theology* (Grand Rapids: Eerdmans, December 1969), 204.

[4] Keil and Delitzsch, *Commentaries,* 1:133.

[5] Ibid., 1:134.

[6] Jacob A. Loewen, "Language: Vernacular, Trade, or National?" *Readings in Missionary Anthropology II,* ed. William A. Smalley (Pasadena: William Carey, 1978), 664.

[7] Ibid., 664.

[8] David Hesselgrave, *Communicating Christ Cross-Culturally* (Grand Rapids: Zondervan, 1978), 246, 250.

[9] Harris Winitz, *Learnables,* Vols. 1–4 (Kansas City: International Linguistics, 1990).

Chapter 3

[1] These are seed thoughts for cross-cultural workers whose primary ministry is telling the Story. Those who focus primarily on relief and development will have a much broader background in the material presented in this chapter.

[2] John Paton, *Thirty Years with South Sea Cannibals: Autobiography of John G. Paton* (Chicago: Moody, 1964), 188–204.

[3] Gordon Wetmore, "A Contemporary View of the Book of Acts and Its Relationship to People in Need or, Little Ones to Him Belong," *AERDO Occasional Paper # 1* (Washington, D.C.: AERDO, n.d.), 1, 7.

[4] John Stott, *Christian Mission in the Modern World* (London: IVP, 1976), 27.

[5] Roland Allen, *Missionary Methods: St. Paul's or Ours?* (Grand Rapids: Eerdmans, 1972), 49.

[6] Roland Bunch, *Two Ears of Corn: A Guide to People-Centered Agricultural Improvement* (Oklahoma City: World Neighbors: 1982), 14.

[7] Rich Campbell, *The Christ of the Korean Heart* (Columbus: Falcon, 1954), 144.

[8] "If Ever a Country Cried out for Conflict Resolution," *Mennonite Weekly Review* 77 (July 2, 1998), 27.

[9] Ibid., 28. Italics in original.

[10] Alain Peyrefitte, *Le Mal Français* (Paris: France Loisirs, 1976), 4–5.

[11] William van Geest, "Development and Other Religious Activities," *Together,* No. 55 (July-September, 1997), 4.

Chapter 4

[1] Louis Bobé, *Hans Egede: Colonizer and Missionary to Greenland* (Copenhagen: Rosenkilde and Bagger, 1952) quoted in Ruth A. Tucker, *From Jerusalem to Irian Jaya* (Grand Rapids: Zondervan, 1983), 78.

[2] Joseph H. Thayer, *Thayer's Greek-English Lexicon of the New Testament* (Grand Rapids: Baker, 1977). All Greek word definitions in this chapter are based on Thayer's Lexicon.

[3] ALPHA courses, Holy Trinity Brompton, Brompton Rd., London, UK, SW7 1JA (www.alpha.org.uk). A similar method is described in *Mission Possible: implantation d'églises dans une Europe post-chrétienne* by Johan Lukasse (Editions Emmaüs, 1993), which is successfully being used in Belgium to plant churches.

[4] "Presstime Prayerlines," *Alliance Life* (March 12, 1997), 3.

[5] Ibid. (May 21, 1997), 3.

Chapter 5

[1] This story is true, but names have been changed.

[2] David Hesselgrave, *Communicating Christ Cross-Culturally* (Grand Rapids: Zondervan, 1978), 233–234.

[3] John R. W. Stott, *Christian Mission in the Modern World* (Downers Grove: IVP, 1976), 126.

[4] James F. Engel, *How to Communicate the Gospel Effectively* (Achimota, Ghana: African Christian Press, 1988).

[5] John Milton Gregory, *The Seven Laws of Teaching* (Grand Rapids: Baker 1967), 67–68.

[6] Gordon Hedderly Smith, *The Blood Hunters* (Chicago: World Wide Prayer & Missionary League, 1942), 69.

[7] Donald McGavran, *Understanding Church Growth* (Grand Rapids: Eerdmans, 1970), 297.

[8] Eugeniy N. Nedzelskiy, "The Protestant Crisis in Russia," *Evangelical Missions Quarterly,* 34:3 (July 1998), 292–297.

[9] H. L. Richard, "Is Extraction Evangelism Still the Way to God?" *Mission Frontiers Bulletin,* 18:9–10 (September-October 1996), 15.

[10] Hesselgrave, *Communicating Christ,* 240–241.

[11] This is a true story, but names have been changed.

Chapter 6

[1] "Church" refers to the universal Church of followers of Christ, whereas "church" describes a local assembly of followers or a regional group of assemblies.

[2] Tom Julien, "The Essence of the Church," *Evangelical Missions Quarterly*, 34:2 (April 1998), 150.

[3] Peter Beyerhaus, "The Three Selves Formula: Is it on biblical foundations?" in *Reading in Dynamic Indigeneity,* eds. C. Kraft and T. Wisely (Pasadena: William Carey Library, 1979), 15–30.

[4] The foreign worker often describes the local congregation established in the foreign country to which he is sent as the "national church." It nicely distinguishes the new congregation(s) from his sending assembly, called the "home church." As will be seen, the foreign or national church is not the only congregation that is a "national" church.

[5] Note the passages in Acts that describe evangelism that was practiced by every believer: 2:41–43; 5:42; 6:7; 8:4, 12; 9:31; 11:21; 12:24; 13:39; 14:21; 19:20.

[6] Pedro Aruppe, "Letter to the Society of Jesus on Inculturation," 9, as quoted in "Christology, Inculturation, and their Missiological Implications: A Latin American Perspective," in *International Bulletin of Missionary Research*, 28:2 (April 2004), 61.

[7] Howard Snyder, *Signs of the Spirit: How God Reshapes the Church* (Grand Rapids: Zondervan, 1989).

[8] This story is a composite of many similar experiences of spontaneous church growth. The books by Mike Berg, C. Peter Wagner, and William Read provide helpful information about the exceptionally fast growth of the church in Latin America.

Chapter 7

[1] This story is a composite, with names and places changed.

[2] Frank Fortunato, "Trends in Global Worship: Charting the Progress Toward the Realization of Revelation 5:13," *Mission Frontiers Bulletin,* 18:5–8 (May-August 1996), 25.

[3] Dave Hall, "Taking Worship to the Nations: Three Biblical Principles to Guide us Into Worship Renewal Among the Nations," *Mission Frontiers Bulletin,* 18:5–8 (May-August 1996), 28–30.

[4] J. Bolton and C. Stacey Woods, "Our Hope" (InterVarsity Christian Fellowship, March 1946), quoted by A. P. Hay, *The New Testament Order for Church and Missionary* (Welland, Ont., Canada: New Testament Missionary Union, 1947), 321.

[5] Donald McGavran, *Momentous Decisions in Missions Today* (Grand Rapids: Baker, 1984), 44.

[6] Arch Campbell, *The Christ of the Korean Heart* (Columbus: Falcon, 1954), 12.

Chapter 8

[1] The letter was written by a Christian in Anhui, China, to Trans World Radio. Taken from *Trans World Radio: Listeners' Letters* (PR301797).

[2] Note these passages indicating the importance of training leaders as gifts emerge—Acts 6:1–4; 13:1–4; 20:7ff; 2 Tim. 1:13–14; 2 Tim. 2:14–16.

[3] Isobel S. Kuhn, *In the Arena* (Chicago: Moody, 1958), 129–158.

[4] William A. Smalley, *Readings in Dynamic Indigeneity* (Pasadena: William Carey library, 1979), 35.

[5] Ibid., 39.

[6] This is a true story. Names and places have been withheld for security.

Chapter 9

[1] David H. Moore, *Missiological Principles,* paper presented to the members of the Department of Overseas Ministries of the Christian and Missionary Alliance, August 2–4, 1988. I am indebted to Mr. Moore for many of these conclusions.

[2] David J. Hesselgrave, *Planting Churches Cross-Culturally* (Grand Rapids: Zondervan, 1980), 408.

[3] L. L. King, letter to author, May 5, 1989.

Chapter 10

[1] Glenn Schwartz, ed., *Transition Notes,* 13 (August 1997).

[2] Please consult the selections noted in Additional Reading, which provide more detail on the topic. It must be understood, however, that the best transition is planned from birth.

[3] A helpful book for transition of training institutes is *Able to Teach Others Also* by William H. Smallman (Pasadena: Mandate Press, 2001).

[4] A helpful dissertation on the subject of transitioning to other ministries, included in the Additional Reading list, is *Transition that Enables the Church to Stand Strong* by Robert Fetherlin (Deerfield: Trinity International University, 1998).

[5] Alan R. Tippett, "Indigenous Principles in Mission Today," in *Readings in Dynamic Indigeneity,* eds: Charles H. Kraft and Tom N. Wisley (Pasadena: William Carey Library, 1979), 69. Quotation marks as in original.

Chapter 11

[1] Eileen Crossman, *Mountain Rain: A New Biography of James O. Fraser* (Southampton, UK: Camelot Press for OMF Books, 1982), 130–133.

[2] Glenn Schwartz, "Don't Chase Buffaloes," in *WMA Perspectives* (Spring 1993).

[3] Daryl Anderson, the European Director of the Evangelical Free Church Overseas Missions, wrote a letter to *EMQ* clarifying this problem of doing church planting in Europe out of the power of American wealth. He said, "We often taught more dependence on material resources from the U.S.A. than dependence on the Lord. This kind of teaching will always come back to haunt us. When we cannot provide all that the nationals want or think they need, we are then resented. We are seen as withholding God's blessings, or accused of selfishness or hoarding. In the end we are not accepted as missionaries when we cease to bring material goods.... A strategy for church planting based only on national resources, will often develop more slowly. But it will build a firm foundation that will last...." In *Evangelical Missions Quarterly,* 31:4 (October 1995), 392–393. I have encountered a similar problem in Western Europe.

[4] Glenn Schwartz states that pervasive spiritual revival at all levels of the church needs to precede a decision for full ownership of their faith. This will make the decision for Christ-reliance a spiritual conviction. See the Additional Reading.

Chapter 12

[1] Howard Taylor, *Hudson Taylor and the China Inland Mission* (London: China Inland Mission, 1958).

² Ibid., 329.

³ Ibid., 331.

⁴ Ibid., 332–336.

⁵ The present imperative verb suggests that we are to be habitually putting on the whole armor. We need it all the time.

⁶ D. A. Carson, *The Cross and Christian Ministry: An Exposition of Passages from 1 Corinthians* (Grand Rapids: Baker, 1993), 25–26.

Additional Reading

¹ World Mission Associates has a series of teaching videos composed from seminars given in Africa on self-reliance. Contact WMA-UK, Box 346, Reading, Berkshire England, RG1 6DH. Also check their website for updated materials: <http://www.wmausa. org>.

About the Author

PAUL AND MARIAN KEIDEL first went to Zaire, Africa, as missionaries with the Christian and Missionary Alliance (C&MA) in 1979, they taught student pastors and wives at Kinkonzi Bible Institute. Paul mentored student pastors in evangelism and church planting, and partnered with national church leaders to train lay pastors. Marian trained pastors' wives in literacy and Bible study. They led the C&MA ministry team for three years.

In 1989, the Keidels were redeployed to Guinea, West Africa, where they taught at Telekoro Bible Institute. At that time it was the only pastors' training institute in Guinea. With the national church leaders, Paul developed a strategy that brought the Bible School into full church ownership. As the Assistant Field Director couple, Paul and Marian had primary oversight of new missionaries in language study.

The Keidels transitioned to France in 1999, and presently serve as team leaders for the C&MA church-planting team. Marian is involved in a pastoral-care role with women in ministry. Paul also teaches as visiting professor at the Geneva Bible Institute.

Paul was raised in Belgian Congo where his parents served in church planting and literature ministries. He received a BS in Christian Education from Ft. Wayne Bible College (now Taylor University), an M.Div. in pastoral care from Bethel Theological Seminary (St. Paul, MN), and a Doctor of Missiology degree from Trinity International University (Deerfield, IL).

Paul and Marian have been happily married since 1972. Their two adult sons live in the US.

Printed in the United States
56454LVS00002B/91-14

3 4711 00184 7138